I0152390

The Star Messengers

Proclaimers of times and signs

Scripture quotations are taken from the Messianic Study Bible © 2018 or King James Version (Note: "Yeshua" is the original Hebrew pronunciation of the name of Jesus).

When traditions and historical events from apocryphal books are credible and also supported by historical records, then they are used as supporting evidence.

Images: The abbreviation "WC" refers to Wikimedia Commons, a public domain source. Astronomical images I did myself using *Stellarium*. The "celestial clock" images I also did myself (on GIMP). (I'm writing in the first person when I make comments or refer to myself, it is more natural I think)

Internet addresses (websites, blogs, etc.) printed in this booklet are offered as a resource to you. These are not intended in any way to be or imply an endorsement on my part .

Astronomical events are based on observations from the Middle East in the time of Jesus. Due to astronomical phenomena the times change for certain events (e.g. the dates for the heliacal rising and setting of stars). Dates, unless specifically stated otherwise, is according to the Gregorian calendar.

Cover design by Gerhard Groenewald

Printed and bound in South Africa by Bidvest Data, Cape Town.
Also available on Amazon.com

ISBN 978-0-6399999-0-6

MOADIM
MEDIA

Published by Moadim Media

Soli Deo Gloria

Glory to God alone.
Without Him this book would not be possible.

I dedicate this book to my mother.
A special word of thanks to everybody
who supported me and prayed for me.

Thank you for your trust in me.
Blessings and shalom to you all!

Foreword: Does it really matter?

The themes and messages of the appointed times teach us more about Jesus Christ: who he is, what he came to do and what he still will do. According to the Bible he was born on an appointed time, and he also died on an appointed time:

> Gal 4:4a but when the appointed time came, God sent forth his Son.

> 1Tim 2:5+6 For there is one God, and one mediator between God and men, the man Yeshua the Messiah; who gave himself as a ransom for all, the witness at the appointed time.

We believe that he is also coming back on an appointed time:

> 1Th 4:16 For the Lord himself shall descend from heaven with a shout, with the voice of the archangel, and with the trump of God; and the dead in the Messiah shall rise first.

The "Trump of God" refers to Yom Teruah (Feast of Trumpets), one of the appointed times in the Bible.

The Hebrew word "moadim"[1] means "appointed times". It refers to anything that happens at a certain time or period. It can be specific dates for appointments (e.g. the so-called "Biblical feasts", which are in fact appointments with God), new moons, the seasons of the year, etcetera.

It is truly amazing how the astronomical events confirm the date of birth of Jesus.

Sha'ul ("Paul") calls the appointed times "foreshadows"; because they are symbolic and prophetic (Col 2:17).

If the "moadim" are about Jesus, then what can we learn about him when we study the appointed time of his birth?

---

[1] The plural of mo'ed is moadim. It is pronounced "mow'ah'deem"

4

Some people believe that if God wanted us to know the date of birth of his Son, then He would have told us. But who says that He didn't? What does the Bible say about the date of birth of Jesus?

Why is there seemingly "irrelevant information" in the Bible that seems redundant, but which is essential to determine the date of the birth of Jesus?

What if it is an end time revelation that points to his return, in order to warn us to be ready?

The astronomical signs at the birth of Jesus also reminds us of the soon-coming return of Jesus.[2] I believe *that* is the reason why God only now made it possible for us to determine the date of birth of his Son.

Furthermore, without some divine revelations this book would have been impossible.

> And God said:
> Let there be lights in the firmament of the heaven,
> to divide the day from the night;
> and let them be for signs,
> and for appointed times and seasons,
> and for days, and years.
>
> Genesis 1:14

---

[2] People who look at the stars to make predictions about the second coming of Jesus ("Astro-prophets") are especially interested in astronomical events in the Leo and Virgo constellations.

Index

Part 3: Calculating the date of birth of Jesus

Part 4: Chronology and significance of dates

---

[3] Modern name is Nissan. Sometimes translated as Abib.

Part 5: Ages and dispensations

Part 6: Controversial / debatable issues

Appendixes

Part 1: Astronomy and calendars

Origins of civilization: The "Out of Africa" hoax

In the 1940's a skull fossil was found at the Sterkfontein caves near Johannesburg in South Africa. It was named "Mrs Ples". Some paleontologists then claimed that it is "evidence" that humans originated there, so they called the area the *Cradle of Humankind* (UNESCO declared it a *World Heritage Site* in 1999).

But their theory (which was taken as fact) was never proven. Some scientists have questioned or rejected the *Out of Africa* theory, and with good reasons:

1. More fossils were found at different places. Each one was claimed by some paleontologists and anthropologists to be the oldest (usually by the person/s who found them!):
    a. The *Jebel Irhoud* skull from Morocco (found in 1961).
    b. The *Ndutu* skull from Tanzania (found in 1973).
    c. The *Bodo* skull from Ethiopia (found in 1976) and
    d. The *Dali* skull from China (found in 1978).

    (So where will the next "oldest" skull fossil be found?)

2. Historical, archeological and linguistic evidence support the case that humans originated from Mesopotamia.

3. Genetic studies[4] have actually disproven the *Out of Africa* theory:

Klyosov and Rozhanskii (2012:80) say the following:

---

[4] Klyosov, A. & Rozhanskii, I. (2012). Re-Examining the "Out of Africa" Theory and the Origin of Europeoids (Caucasoids) in Light of DNA Genealogy. *Advances in Anthropology, 2*, 80-86. doi: 10.4236/ aa.2012.22009. Online (24/10/2018): [http://www.scirp.org/journal/PaperInformation.aspx?PaperID=19566]

Klyosov, A. (2014). Reconsideration of the "Out of Africa" Concept as Not Having Enough Proof. *Advances in Anthropology, 4*, 18-37. doi: 10.4236/aa. 2014.41004. Online (10/2018):
[http://www.scirp.org/journal/PaperInformation.aspx?PaperID=42557]

"Moreover, a genomic gap exists between some Africans and non-Africans, which has also been interpreted as an argument that the latter descended from Africans. A more plausible interpretation might have been that both current Africans and non-Africans descended separately from a more ancient common ancestor, thus forming a proverbial fork".

Typical tree diagrams of the Y-haplogroup of the world clearly show that the A and B Y-DNA haplogroups are separate branches, and that other Y-haplogroups DO NOT come from them.

DNA genealogy is based on some assumed theoretical foundations. Theories should always be taught as possibilities only. Those that have been proven to be untrue should be discarded (which unfortunately almost never happens).

Mesopotamia: The REAL Cradle of Mankind

Gen 11:1-2 And the whole earth was of one language, and of one speech. And it came to pass, as they journeyed from the east, that they found a plain in the land of Shinar; and they dwelt there.

Historians have always believed that the cradle of mankind is in Mesopotamia, because that is what the archeological evidence clearly show. Almost all of the more than 200 flood legends around the world say that there was a global flood (this is also confirmed by *flood geology* and *Mitochondrial DNA[5]*).

In most of them the survivors were a family in a boat that ended up on a mountain (The ancient Chinese symbol for flood is a pictograph of 8 people on a boat). There are also extra-Biblical records of the tower of Babel and the subsequent dispersion of people from there.

---

[5] http://www.icr.org/article/new-dna-study-confirms-noah/

The origins of astronomy and calendars

Time is the result of matter moving through space. Our clocks and calendars are based on or derived from observations of one or more celestial bodies.

The ancient *Mayan Long Count calendar* had a solar year of 365 days called *Haab*. People must have had a good astronomical understanding to devise that. It started in 3114 BC, during the life of the prophet Enoch. It seems that he was the father of astronomy and the solar calendar:

- According to Biblical chronology he lived for 365 years (c.3338 BC to c.2973 BC). There seems to be a connection.
- "Enoch calendars" have months of 30 days - just like the ancient solar calendars of 365 days.
- The *Mayan solar calendar* of 365 days started during his lifetime.
- According to Eupolemus[6] Enoch invented astronomy.

Enoch taught Methuselah (Noah's grandfather) and Lamech (Noah's father), and they taught Noah. Noah followed a solar calendar with 30 day months (Gen 7:11+24 and 8:3-4).

It most probably had an extra 5 days at the end, like many ancient solar calendars. The Chaldeans, Medes, Persians, Egyptians, Grecians, Romans and even Mexicans had these 5 days at the end of their civil year. It was a time of feasting.

Many ancient cultures had two calendars: A civil solar calendar and a religious lunisolar calendar. The lunisolar religious calendar consisted of 12 lunar months, plus an extra intercalary month inserted by decree when needed[7].

---

[6] Eupolemus, cited in Eusebius (c.320 CE). *Praeparatio Evangelica 9.17.8*

[7] The Babylonian Empire later adopted this "Umma calendar of Shulgi". Shulgi was a great Sumerian king, 2029-1982 BC). Their year began in spring in the month *Nissanu*, on the first new moon after the vernal equinox. During their Babylonian exile the Jews started to call the first Biblical month *Nissan* instead of *Aviv*.

Nimrod, the Sumerians, Chaldeans and Babylonians

The Sumerians were pioneers of astronomy and astrology more than 4000 years ago. They had written records of astronomical observations going back to 2234 BC:

Callisthenes, the philosopher who accompanied Alexander the Great when he took possession of Babylon in 331 BC, found records of astronomical observations going back 1903 years. He sent the records to Aristotle in Greece (they were relatives).[8]

The Chinese and Egyptian astronomical accounts support these old astronomical observations. There is evidence of a common origin of the Chaldean and Egyptian astronomy.[9]

Gen 10:6+8 And the sons of Cham/Ham: Cush (aka Bel or Belus), Mizraim (Egypt) and Put and Canaan. And Cush begat Nimrod: he began to be a mighty one in the earth.

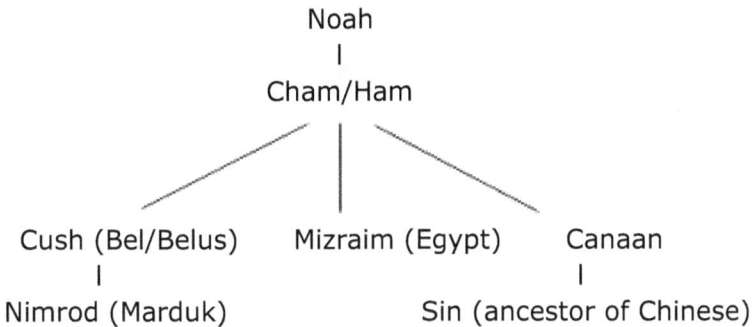

Noah
|
Cham/Ham

Cush (Bel/Belus)	Mizraim (Egypt)	Canaan
Nimrod (Marduk)		Sin (ancestor of Chinese)

It is believed that Cham delivered the knowledge of astronomy to Cush and Nimrod after the flood.

---

[8] Simplicius of Cilicia (c. 535 AD), *Ad Aristotle De Caelo*, lib. ii. p. 123 (About the heavens) (His commentary on Aristotle's cosmological treatise *De Caelo*, 350 BC). Porphyry (an anti-Christian Greek philosopher, c. 234–305 AD) said the same in his *Simplicium In De Caelo*.

[9] William Hales (1830). *A new analysis of chronology and geography, history and prophecy*, Volume 1 (Gilbert and Rivington, London). p37 - 40
John Jackson (1752). *Chronological Antiquities Or The Antiquities and Chronology of the most ancient kingdoms*, Vol 2 (Printed by J.Noon, London). P76

According to the Bible Cham was the ancestor of the Sumerians (the Cushites who lived there), the Egyptians and the Chinese - the three ancient civilizations who were the pioneers and leaders of astronomy (and unfortunately also of astrolatry).

The Chinese are descendants of Sin. He was a son of Canaan, and Canaan was a son of Cham (or Ham), a son of Noah (Gen 10:6+15+17). China is still called *Sin* in Hebrew (The plural of Chinese in Hebrew is *Sinim*, as it is written in Isa 49:12).

The capital of the Sumerians was Ur. The Gudea cylinders (circa 2125 BC, about 80 years after the flood) are clay cylinders with Sumerian text in cuneiform script. They contain references to constellations and stars.

Nimrod re-established astrology and sun worship in the post-flood world. Nimrod is represented by the constellation Orion. Because of their obvious connection with the seasons they considered the stars to be gods and worshipped them. This is called astrolatry.

According to Josephus[10] it was Nimrod (Marduk[11]) who built the tower of Babel. Historians reckon that it was actually a ziggurat that was used as a temple and astronomical observatory.

> *Gen 11:3-4 And they said one to another, Go to, let us make brick, and burn them thoroughly. And they had brick for stone, and slime had they for mortar. And they said: Go to, let us build us a city and a tower, whose top may reach unto heaven; and let us make us a name, lest we be scattered abroad upon the face of the whole earth.*

The words "*whose top may reach unto heaven*" (Gen 11:4) does not mean that they wanted to build a tower that literally reached into the clouds, but rather that they wanted to build a *gateway* or *portal* to the spiritual dimension/heaven.

---

[10] Josephus, F (c.94 CE). *Jewish Antiquities 1.4*

[11] Nimrod is associated with Marduk. See *Names and associations of deities* on page 133.

Ziggurats were built as doorways for "*gods*" to approach man, in other words invoking demons (The word *Babel* comes from the Akkadian *bab-ili* which means *gate of God*).

In c.2202[12] BC there was an earthquake, at the time of the dispersion of the people (Gen 10:25). When Belus II became king he repaired the tower of Babel and built an observatory thereon.

The ancient Chaldeans were descendents of the Sumerians. The Chaldeans inherited their knowledge of astronomy and further developed it. Later they became part of the Babylonian Empire (they even ruled it for some time). They played the leading role in their astronomy and astrology. The word "Chaldeans" became associated with Babylonian astronomers/ astrologers.

The Babylonians had advanced knowledge of mathematics. They did astronomical calculations using arithmetic and geometrical mathematics. Ancient Babylonian clay tablets[13] (dated between 1800 BC and 1600 BC) show that they were familiar with the Pythagoras[14] Theorem $(x^2+y^2 = r^2)$, which is fundamental in geometry and trigonometry.

---

[12] Some sceptics say that 100 years after the flood was not enough time for the people to have increased enough so that they could build the tower. That is not true. The ziggurats were built with burned bricks. They were not as big as the pyramids, more like a big public building.

A team of 140 workers can build a ziggurat. One worker can make 1000 clay bricks by hand per day. One bricklayer can lay 1000 bricks per day. One team of 140 workers can have 10 bricklayers that lay 10000 bricks per day.

The average age of a generation is 25. Some fathers (like Joktan) had up to 13 sons. The three sons of Noah had 16 sons. If we take an average of 5 sons per father for 4 generations, then we get at least 2000 males after 100 years (16x5x5x5).

[13] Plimpton tablet 322, Yale tablet YBC 7289, the Susa tablet and the Tell Dhibayi tablet

[14] Pythagoras (c.569 BC – c.490 BC), usually credited for this theorem, was born more than a 1000 years later.

Abraham and astronomy

Abraham came from Ur of the Chaldeans. They were a civilisation with advanced astronomical knowledge. Abraham and his family served idols (Jos 24:2). If Abraham's father was a pagan priest (as is believed), then they would have had knowledge of astronomy.

Apparently Abraham was a great astronomer and scientist who used astronomy to prove God's existence. According to tradition Noah and Shem taught him true science and the worship of the Most High God. We read in the Apocryphal Book of Jasher of how Abraham stayed with them, and how he came to realize that celestial bodies are not gods (Jas 9:5-19).

Josephus wrote[15]: "Berosus[16] mentions our father Abram without naming him, when he says thus: "*In the tenth generation after the Flood, there was among the Chaldeans a man righteous and great, and skillful in the celestial science.*" Josephus wrote further: "But Hecataeus does more than barely mention him; for he composed, and left behind him, a book concerning him ... Now the name of Abram is even still famous in the country of Damascus; and there is shown a village named from him, *The Habitation of Abram.*"

Eusebius quoted Josephus quoting Besorus as follows[17]: "*In the tenth generation after the flood there was among the Chaldeans a righteous and great man, experienced also in heavenly things.*"

The Bible states that Abraham was a righteous man, and that he was born into the 10th generation after the Flood (Gen 11, 15:6, 26:5, Heb 11:8).

A stellium occurs when 4 or more planets are located in the same sign. According to astrologers stelliums are astronomical events that will significantly change the world. Astronomical events don't really cause the change (like the astrologers believe), but they are signs that something did happen or is going to happen (Gen 1:14).

---

[15] Josephus, F (c.94 CE). *Jewish Antiquities 1.7.2*
[16] Berosus was a Chaldean historian from the 3rd century BC
[17] Eusebius (c.320 CE). *Praeparatio Evangelica 9.1*

Abraham's Birth: A Great Event

On 26 February 1953 BC there was a 5 planet stellium in Aquarius. This was an extremely rare event: All 5 visible planets were located within 4.33° - the tightest grouping of the five visible planets in a period of 8020 years![18]

Abraham would be regarded in very great esteem if he was born during that stellium - and apparently he was! He was born about 1951 vC, based on Biblical chronology. But months are often not included in Biblical timelines, so it is more likely that he actually was born in 1953 vC. The Book of Jasher describes a star "swallowing up" 4 other stars on the night when Abraham was born (Jas 8:1-4). That is a good description of that stellium.

That stellium indeed did signal a momentous change in the world: The birth of Abraham ushered in the Age of the Ram (Aries). It was clearly demonstrated with the ram that he sacrificed on Mount Moriah (Gen 22).

The Babylonian astrologers were in service of the royal court. They studied astronomy so that they could predict eclipses and the movement of Jupiter. Jupiter was associated with Marduk (Zeus), their chief god. They used their knowledge of astronomy to deceive the people into thinking that that they were communicating with their deities.

Abraham was more logical in his reasoning: he came to the conclusion that if the celestial bodies followed fixed paths that could be predicted, then they had no free will of their own and were not gods.

If their paths were predetermined then there had to be One who controlled them, and that One could only be the Creator.

---

[18] The Free Library (2014). *Conjunctions That Changed the World : The conjunction of May 2000 is an occasion for looking back at planetary groupings that have changed history.*
Online (09/2018):
[https://www.thefreelibrary.com/Conjunctions+That+Changed+the+World+%3a+The+conjunction+of+May+2000+is...-a061591263]

The new faith of Abraham was a threat to the pagan priests, so they chased him away, according to the apocryphal book Judith (KJV):

Jdt 5:8 For they left the way of their ancestors, and worshipped the God of heaven, the God whom they knew: so they cast them out from the face of their gods, and they fled into Mesopotamia, and sojourned there many days.

Jdt 5:9a Then their God commanded them to depart from the place where they sojourned, and to go into the land of Canaan.

It says that "**they** *left the way of their ancestors*". Both Abraham and his father Terach turned to Yahweh, the True God.

This is supported by the fact that Terach took his family and left Ur of the Chaldees:

Gen 11:31 And Terach took Abram his son, and Lot the son of Haran his son's son, and Sarai his daughter in law, his son Abram's wife; and they went forth with them from Ur of the Chaldees, to go into the land of Canaan; and they came unto Haran, and dwelt there.

In the following verse Laban called the God of Abraham also the God of the father of Abraham and his brother Nachor[19]:

Gen 31:53 The God (Elohim) of Abraham, and the God (Elohim) of Nachor, the God (Elohim) of their father, judge between us. And Jacob swore by the fear of his father Isaac.

There was famine in Canaan so Abraham went to Egypt (Gen 12:10).

---

[19] Some commentators say that Laban referred to two different gods. But a similar language structure is used in the following verse which clearly refers to one God:

Exo 3:15 And God said moreover unto Moshe: Thus shall thou say unto the children of Israel: Yahweh, the God of your fathers, the God of Abraham, the God of Isaac, and the God of Jacob, has sent me unto you: this is my name for ever, and this is my memorial unto all generations.

Abraham and Egyptian astronomy and arithmetic

Apparently Abraham taught the Egyptians astronomy and arithmetic:

Josephus[20]: "He communicated to them arithmetic, and delivered to them the science of astronomy; for before Abram came into Egypt they were unacquainted with those parts of learning; for that science came from the Chaldeans into Egypt, and from thence to the Greeks also".

Eupolemus[21]: "And Abraham dwelt with the Egyptian priests in Heliopolis and taught them many things. It was he who introduced astronomy and the other sciences to them, saying that the Babylonians and himself had found these things out, but tracing back the first discovery to Enoch, and saying that he, and not the Egyptians, had first invented astrology".

Artapanus[22]: "Abraham ... with all his household came into Egypt, to the Egyptian king Pharethothes and taught him astrology."

There is archeological evidence that supports what they wrote:

Anderson[23]: "In a revised chronology, Abraham would have visited Egypt when Khufu (aka Cheops) was Pharaoh. Before Khufu, the early Egyptian pyramids were fantastic architectural structures, but they were not perfectly square or exactly oriented to all four points on a compass. However, when Khufu built his masterful pyramid, there appears to have been an explosion of astronomical and mathematical expertise. Khufu's pyramid was perfectly square, level, and orientated to the four points of the compass.

When placed in the proper dynasty, Abraham's visit to Egypt may have been the catalyst that sparked an architectural revolution in Egyptian history."

---

[20] Josephus, F (c.94 CE). *Jewish Antiquities 1.8.2*
[21] Eupolemus, cited in Eusebius (c.320 CE). *Praeparatio Evangelica 9.17.8*
[22] Artapanus, cited in Eusebius (c.320 CE). *Praeparatio Evangelica 9.18:1*
  [http://www.ccel.org/ccel/pearse/morefathers/files/eusebius_pe_09_book9.htm]
[23] Daniel Anderson (2007). Egyptian history and the biblical record: a perfect match?
  [https://creation.com/egyptian-history-and-the-biblical-record-a-perfect-match]

Astronomical time units

Job 38:31+32 Can thou bind the sweet influences of Pleiades, or loose the bands of Orion? Can thou bring forth the constellations in their season? or can thou guide Arcturus with his sons?

Months

The astronomical new moon (Heb.: "Molad") is the first phase of the moon cycle. It takes place at the moment when the Moon comes between the earth and the sun (same ecliptic longitude). The Moon is then not visible because its illuminated side is showing away from us. The Biblical month is from new moon to new moon.

Lunisolar years

A lunisolar calendar consists of 12 lunar months, plus an intercalary month inserted by decree when needed (in order to keep the year to the seasons). Some ancient civilizations (e.g. the Sumerians/ Chaldeans / Babylonians and the Chinese[24]) followed the metonic cycle, with 7 intercalary months in a course of 19 years. The Jewish lunisolar calendar of today is based on the metonic cycle.

Solar or tropical years

A solar year is the time that it takes the sun to return to the same position in the cycle of seasons; e.g. from vernal equinox to vernal equinox. It is also called a *tropical* year, from the Greek word *tropikos* which means "to turn".

This is the year that our modern calendar is based on. It is about 365,242 days long.

Sidereal or star years

A sidereal year is the time it takes for the earth and sun to return to the same position with respect to the fixed stars. Astronomers use this "star year calendar" because it enables them to easily point their telescopes to the proper coordinates in the night sky.

---

[24] John Jackson (1752). *Chronological Antiquities Or The Antiquities and Chronology of the most ancient kingdoms*, Vol 2 (Printed by J.Noon, London). p.66

A sidereal year is about 365.256 days long (about 20 minutes longer than a solar year). A sidereal day is about 4 minutes shorter than a normal day, which means that the sidereal year has an extra sidereal day. This also causes the beginning of the sidereal day to start every day at a different time.

Some ancient calendars (e.g. the Indian Tamil calendar) are based on the sidereal year. The word *sidereal* comes from the Latin *sidus* that means "star".

Years and the heliacal risings and settings of stars

Stars seen from the poles are always above the horizon. They are called *circumpolar*. No star observed at the equator is circumpolar, they all rise and set. Some stars observed at places between the poles and the equator rise and set, while others are circumpolar.

The stars seem to move faster than the sun when we observe them (they rise about 4 minutes earlier per day). That is because of the difference between the tropical and sidereal solar year. If it was not for this phenomena, some stars would always be near the sun and never be visible outside the Arctic Circle.

The word *heliacal* means "pertaining to the sun". It comes from the Greek word *helios* which means "the sun". When stars are in conjunction with the sun (near the sun, as observed from earth) they are not visible.

When a star becomes visible again after its invisibility we call it the *heliacal rising* of that star. The last sighting of the star, before it becomes invisible again because of its conjunction with the sun, is called the *heliacal setting* of that star. This is usually on the same day of the year.[25] This date moves slowly because of the precession of the equinoxes (caused by the difference between the solar and sidereal/star year).

---

[25] Dates for heliacal events are dependent on visible observations which are influenced by atmospheric conditions. Different sources give different dates, depending on the chosen parameters for visibility that are used in their calculations. For the purpose of this book the "average dates" were chosen as the most probable ones.

Seasons and calendars

Seasons occur because of the tilt of the earth's rotational axis. As the earth move around the sun, the direct rays of the sun (when it is directly above) move between the tropics. This causes the different seasons.

> Gen 8:22 While the earth remains, seedtime and harvest, cold and heat, and summer and winter, and day and night shall not cease.

Many ancient cultures had two calendars: A civil solar (tropical or sidereal) calendar and a religious and agricultural lunisolar calendar. Many cultures used the tropical solar calendar of 365 days as their civil calendar. The beginning of the year was not fixed to any specific season and slowly moved between them.

The beginning of the lunisolar calendar is fixed to one of the seasons. Different cultures have used different seasons for the start dates. Intercalary months are added where necessary. This calendar is used to determine religious festivals. The seasons for planting and harvesting stay more or less in the same months.

The sidereal star calendar is the only truly fixed calendar. It has no leap days or intercalary months. Seasons and religious festivals are always at the same time of year.

Equinoxes and solstices

The equinoxes occur when the sun crosses the celestial equator at the intersection between the celestial equator and the ecliptic plane. The direct rays of the sun are   hen shining on the equator. Day and night are of equal lengths on that day (as reflected in the name).

During the solstices the sun seems to stand still on one of the tropics, before it reverses its direction. The word solstice comes from the Latin word *solstitium*, which means, "the sun stands still". This happens on the longest and shortest day of the year.

The equinoxes and solstices are events that mark the beginning of the seasons from an astronomical perspective.

Astronomical events and the seasons

Spring was confirmed by the "spring stars". They were visible for the whole night during the month of March.[26] The heliacal risings or settings of certain stars were also indications of seasons

Spring	- Spring/Vernal Equinox	20/21 March
"Spring star"	- Tsemech visible the whole night	March
Summer	- Summer Solstice	22/23 June
	- Heliacal rising of Sirius	middle of July
(end of summer)	- Heliacal setting of Tsemech	end of August
Fall/autumn	- Autumnal Equinox	22/23 September
Winter	- Winter Solstice	20/21 December

Autumn:

Many cultures started their year in autumn, after the heliacal setting of Tsemech. This was the season to plow and sow.

Spring:

The Jewish and Babylonian calendars started on the first new moon after the vernal equinox. Spring was the lambing season and the time for the barley harvest.

Tsemech was one of the **spring stars**. Although it could be seen on most nights of the year, by March it could be seen during the whole night.

The Roman calendar started on the 1st of March. For them it was the season to **march** to war. The month March is named after their god of war, Mars.

Summer:

The Egyptian year started with the heliacal rising of Sirius[27] in July. It heralded the flooding of the Nile, after which they planted.

---

[26] Seasons in the Southern Hemisphere are the opposite.

[27] Animation at [http://astro.unl.edu/classaction/animations/ancientastro/heliacalrisingsim.html]

The Vernal Equinox and April fools day

March was the first month in the Roman calendar. It was always the month during which the vernal equinox occurred. The names of the numerical months of our modern calendar are a reminder of this ancient calendar (e.g. September was the 7th month, etcetera)

In 46 BC Julius Caesar changed the lunisolar calendar into a solar calendar, the Julian calendar. New Year's Day was moved back two months (from 1 March to 1 January). The 10th month (December) became the 12th month but retained its name.

In the 3rd century AD the vernal equinox was on 21 March. They used the Julian calendar. The Julian and Gregorian (extrapolated) calendars are the same from 1 Mar 200 AD to 28 Feb 300 AD. The Gregorian calendar has 3 less leap years than the Julian calendar over a 400 year period.

In time the date of 21 March on the Julian calendar moved away from the real date of the vernal equinox.

During the Middle Ages many European countries (e.g. Britain) stopped celebrating New Year's Day on 1 January and started to celebrate it on 25 March. They used the Julian calendar. They did this for religious reasons. They believed that 25 March was the day on which the mother of Jesus became pregnant.

When Pope Gregory instituted the Gregorian calendar in 1582 the beginning of the year was moved back to 1 January.

By that time 25 March of the Julian calendar fell on 1 April on the Gregorian calendar.

Those who cling to the old Julian calendar and new year (25 March) celebrated their new year's day on the 1st of April, according to the Gregorian calendar. In an effort to "convince" them to stop celebrating their new year on 1 April, people started to mock them and making fools out of them.

The Antikythera Mechanism

In 1901 a group of sponge divers discovered a huge shipwreck off the island of Antikythera with many archaeological treasures. One of the objects that they recovered was a mysterious clock-like mechanism. The first studies showed that it was a complex astronomical instrument. It was called the "Antikythera Mechanism".

It is probably the best and clearest example of the link between astronomy, time and calendars. Its an ancient Greek "analogue computer" that used differential gearing (something that people thought were only invented in the 16 century).

WC: Mogi Vicentini, 2007

An interpretative reconstruction of the Antikythera mechanism. The original bronze remains of the device are now in the National Archaeological Museum in Athens.

It is considered to be the world's oldest analogue computer. It is dated to be from the 2nd century BC. It had dials on both sides of the device.

It was used to show the motion of the Moon, sun and planets when the handle was turned.

Only a very intelligent person with advanced knowledge of astronomy and mathematics could design such a sophisticated device.

It was investigated for decades, but only during the last half of the previous century has research begun to reveal its secrets. Highly advanced techniques became available at the beginning of this century. An international team was formed which started the *Antikythera Mechanism Research Project* (*AMRP*) in 2005.

These are their findings:

Overview: "The Antikythera Mechanism is now understood to be dedicated to astronomical phenomena and operates as a complex mechanical "computer" which tracks the cycles of the Solar System".

Tony Freeth: "Our research shows that the Mechanism was even more sophisticated than previously thought, with a remarkable ingenuity of design".

Robert Hannah: "Although now recognised more as a planetarium or orrery, the Antikythera Mechanism was originally identified by Price as a "calendar computer", and despite our present concerns with its sophisticated means of predicting lunar positions and eclipses, it still offers abundant means of marking and measuring time.

This it was able to do in terms of the Egyptian calendar and a parapegma on the front of the dial, and of the Metonic and Callippic lunisolar cycles of 19 and 76 years respectively on the back, where we also now find the Saros and Exeligmos eclipse cycles. Arguably, local civil lunar calendars could also be correlated to the readings from the Mechanism, since it appears that they were still synchronised with the lunar phases.

In its combination of timekeeping methods, the Antikythera Mechanism is very much a product of its times. In the Hellenistic period we find, for instance, the parapegma incorporated into the Egyptian calendar in a festival calendar from Egypt, or the Metonic cycle used as a regulator for the Athenian civil calendar, or sundial and water-clock technology combined in the *Tower of the Winds.*

The sheer variety of timekeeping methods in the one instrument is intriguing, but perhaps the most curious method to modern eyes is the parapegma".

"After a study of the astronomical texts of Ptolemy, Theon Paulus and Heliodorus related to the stationary points of planetary motion, we arrive at the following conclusion: It seems very likely that the Antikythera Mechanism was constructed, apart from other uses,

a) for the observation of the sun, the Moon and (at least) of Venus (possibly other planets also);

b) to model or simulate their longitudinal motions (e.g. only their ecliptic longitude); and

c) in the case of Venus the instrument could also show the stationary points of its path and the retrograde arc between them. The brightness of Venus and its appearance either as morning or evening star may be one but not the only reason for this choice".

"... the signs in both the archaeological record and the historical sources that suggest that the Mechanism is not an isolated development, but indicative of the wider technological context. Although the evidence is scant, there are hints that there may have been working machines with cogs made of bronze. Examples include Heron's dioptra, the barulkos, and the hodometer (which emperor Commodus is alleged to have had on one of his carriages). Machines of an astronomical nature are mentioned several times in the literary sources – the most famous being Archimedes' orrery (Cicero, Republic 14.21; Ovid, Fasti 269-80) – and it seems that "sphere-maker" was a viable occupation in the later Roman Empire...

The evidence suggests that the Antikythera Mechanism was not a solitary phenomenon..."

Conclusion:

Mankind is using the celestial bodies to keep time –
just as God intended when He created them!

AMRP (The Antikythera Mechanism Research Project), *Decoding the Antikythera Mechanism: Science and Technology in Ancient Greece* (Athens, MIET - Cultural Foundation of the National Bank of Greece, 2006)

Part 2: Astronomy and religion

Astronomy plays an important role in in religions. In pagan religions the celestial bodies are worshiped as gods or associated with gods. This is called astrolatry. They are also used for divination in astrology. In Judaism and Christianity they are used to determine the dates for God's appointed times ("Biblical festivals"). God also created them for signs or "star messages" (Gen 1:14).

Celestial bodies and pagan religions

God forbids us to worship any celestial bodies:

> Deu 4:19 And lest thou lift up thine eyes unto heaven, and when thou see the sun, and the moon, and the stars, even all the host of heaven, should be driven to worship them, and serve them, which Yahweh thy God has divided unto all nations[28] under the whole heaven.

> Job 31:26-28 If I beheld the sun when it shined, or the moon walking in brightness; and my heart has been secretly enticed, or my mouth has kissed my hand: This also were an iniquity to be punished by the judge: for I should have denied the God that is above.

One of the most evil kings of Judah was Manasseh, who practiced astrolatry (2Ki 21).

Josiah was a righteous king. He destroyed the pagan altars and put down the idolatrous priests that practiced astrolatry:

> 2 Kng 23:5 And he put down the idolatrous priests, whom the kings of Judah had ordained to burn incense in the high places in the cities of Judah, and in the places round about Jerusalem; them also that burned incense unto Baal, to the sun, and to the moon, and to the planets, and to all the host of heaven.

---

[28] God darkens the minds of people who *don't* want to serve Him, and cause them to worship the creation and not the Creator (Rom 1).

The Shield of David: A "star" that is not a star

Amos 5:26 / Act 7:43 Yea, you took up the tabernacle of Moloch, and the star of your god Chiun (Remphan[29]), figures which you made to worship them...

Some people belief that the verse refers to the "Star of David". But the six pointed "Jewish star" is actually not called a star, it is called the *Shield of David* ("magen Daveed"). It is a sexagram[30], which is a geometrical shape formed by two equilateral triangles placed concentrically on each other.

The 2 triangles of the "magen Daveed" represent the 2 *dalets* in the name of king David. The Hebrew letter *dalet* in ancient paleo-Hebrew is a triangle (The capital Greek letter delta, a triangle, is from the same origin).

The oldest undisputed example of a sexagram is on a seal from the 7th century BC. It was found in Sidon and belonged to one Joshua ben Asayahu. That was after the reign of David and Solomon, and obviously many centuries after the exodus.

The Shield of David is a relatively new Jewish symbol. There is no support in any early rabbinic literature for the claim that it represents the shape or emblem on King David's shield (the symbol is so rare in early Jewish literature and artwork that art dealers suspect forgery if they find the symbol in early works). Theodor Herzl chose the Star of David because it was so well known, and also because it had no religious associations at that time.

In following chapters we will see that the "star of Remphan" was probably the 8-pointed star of Ishtar.

---

[29] "Remphan" is an incorrect transliteration for Chiun, according to the dictionaries

[30] Sometimes a 6 pointed star is shown on artifacts, but it looks like the asterisk sign, not like a sexagram. It represents Nabu, the 3rd son of Marduk, old Mesopotamian deities.

Origin of the Sun and Moon deities

Many pagan practices became part of "Christian" festivals. The worship of celestial bodies is the core of many, if not the most pagan religions, especially sun worship.

The myths that had a big impact on Christmas and Easter celebrations in the Western world can be traced back or reduced to 5 myths:

1. Nimrod/Marduk[31],
2. Isis, her husband Osiris and her son Horus,
3. Tammuz and his wife Ishtar,
4. Deus Sol Invictus Mithras and
5. Saturn the Roman god of agriculture

Deities in one culture were equated with similar deities in other cultures. They usually have more than one name. That can be very confusing. If we put the names of deities in blocks, together with some of their epithets and names of their counterparts, then we can easily follow the common theme of the myths.[32]

Sumerian myth

Marduk / Nimrod (Jupiter)	**Zarpanit**
Chief Babylonian sun god	*Moon goddess*
Other names: Belus, Bel	*Ruler of heaven and earth*
Father of the gods	*Mother of Deities*
King of all the lands	Other names: Beltia, Sharpanitum

---

[31] See "*Names and associations of deities*" on page 133.

[32] Example: Whether you choose Tammuz and Ishtar, or Dumuzid and Inanna, they will tell you more or less the same story. To keep it simple not all the names of all the deities of all the cultures are included.

I'm aware of the possible shortcomings of this diagram. Even if some names are incorrect, the story and the impact of the myth will stay the same. I usually write in the past tense when I'm writing about historical events. Pagan festivals are today celebrated worldwide by neo-Pagans.

Babylonian myth

Tammuz (Saturn)	Ishtar (Venus)
God of storms, fertility & agriculture *God of new life and the seasons* *God of shepherds*	*Queen of Heaven* *Goddess of fertility, Goddess of war* *Goddess of prostitutes and sex*
Sum/Bab: Dumuzid, Tammuz	Sum/Bab: Inanna, Zarpanit, Aphrodite, Asratum,
Sem/Bib: Baal-Hadad, Melqart, Moloch/Baal, Tammuz Egp: Horus Behedet	Sem/Bib: Athirat, Anat, Baalat, Ashertu, Asherah, Ashtoreth Egp: Qetesh, Qudshu, Hathor Qudshu-Astarte-Anat
Greek: Hadad	Greek: Atargatis
Other names: Bacchus, Attis, Adad, Adonis, Adon, Odin, Wodan, Aion, Dionysus, Heracles, Damu	Other names: Artemis, Astare, Astarte, Ashtart, Nanna, Cybele

Egyptian myth

Osiris (Sun)	Isis (Moon)
Other names: Sokar, Kronos, Helios Apollo, Sol, Ra, Ptah-Sokar-Osiris, Apis, Bacchus, Dionysus *God of earth and vegetation*	*Queen of Heaven* Other names: Semiramis, Diana, Ceres, Kore, Proserpina, Persephone, Juno
Seth (brother of Osiris): Baal / Bel *God of storm*	*Goddess with Ten Thousand Names,* *Queen of Heaven, Mother of god*

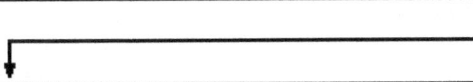

Horus (Orion)	Hathor
Sokar, Harpocrates, Ra-Horakhty "Reincarnation" of Osiris Other names: Helios, Apollo, Sol/Mithras, Ra, Dionysus, Belenos	*Queen of Heaven* *Mother of deities* *Mother of mothers*

Sum/Bab = Sumerian/Babylonian, Sem/Bib = Semitic/Biblical, Egp = Egyptian

Roman myths

Mostly associated with winter solstice festivals in December

Sol	Saturn
Roman sun god	*Roman god of agriculture -*
Sol Indiges, Sol Invictus, Deus Sol Invictus Mithras	Associated with Tammuz and Horus

Nimrod the rebel[33] started it all. He built a temple tower (ziggurat) in the city of Babylon[34]. He was deified as the supreme sun god of the Babylonians. He was often referred to by the title "Bel", which means "lord" or "master" or "owner" (The Semitic form of "Bel" is "Baal").

Sun worship festivals

From midwinter to the beginning of summer various sun worship festivals were held. The birth or rebirth of the sun was celebrated both at the winter solstice and at the vernal equinox.

People believed that their sun god was leaving them in winter because the days were getting shorter. They believed that he returned or was reborn on the winter solstice (20/21 December), because the days were getting longer.

Other "rebirth of the sun" celebrations were in spring. On the vernal equinox day (20/21 March) and night is of equal length, and the days then are getting longer than the nights.

The birth of some deities were celebrated on more than one event. This can be explained by the fact that deities merged. There were at least 4 different falcon gods who were called Horus. They merged and were absorbed by Horus Behedet, who was the most popular.

---

[33] The meaning of his name in Hebrew. See *"Names and associations of deities"* on page 133

[34] Nicole Brisch (2016). 'Marduk (god)', *Ancient Mesopotamian Gods and Goddesses*, Oracc and the UK Higher Education Academy.

[http://oracc.museum.upenn.edu/amgg/listofdeities/marduk/]

Midwinter festivals

11 December: Feast of Sol (Roman)

For the Romans the Sun was the sun god Sol. Every day Sol was racing across the sky with his racing-chariot, drawn by 4 horses, from sunrise to sunset. His birthday was celebrated with chariot-races in the Roman circuses.

On the birthday of Sol the "royal sacrificer" (rex sacrificulus) of the Roman Empire sacrificed a ram to him (This was done only for guardian gods of the Roman state).

It was long thought that Sol Invictus ("Undefeated Sun") and Sol Indiges[35] were different deities, but more recent studies have shown that the Sol Invictus cult was just a continuation of the Sol Indiges cult.[36]

There was a revival of Sol worship in the 1st century AD. It became the chief imperial cult of Rome until it was replaced by Roman Catholicism in 325 AD.

The Roman Mithra and Sol were 2 distinct deities. Roman Mithraism only made its appearance towards the end of the 1st century AD in Rome. This Mithras was not the same as the Iranian one, they only shared a name and, like many other deities, a loose association with the sun.[37]

Eventually these 2 deities merged as *Deus Sol Invictus Mithras*. They moved his birthday to 25 December.[38]

---

[35] A word used for local ("indigenous") deities of Rome.

[36] Hijmans, S. (2010). Temples and Priests of Sol in the City of Rome. Mouseion: *Journal of the Classical Association of Canada*. 10. 381-427. 10.1353/mou.2010.0073. p.2 (PDF)
Online (16/11/2018): [https://www.researchgate.net/publication/242330197_ Temples_and_Priests_of_Sol_in_the_City_of_Rome]

[37] Sources: Mithra vs Jesus [http://tektonics.org/copycat/mithra.php] and http://coldcasechristianity.com/2014/is-jesus-simply-a-retelling-of-the-mithras-mythology

[38] Changed to 25 December in 274 AD in order to coincide with Christmas. See *The 25 December date* on page 124.

In 274 AD the birthday of Sol/Mithras became an official Roman holiday. The emperor Aurelian intentionally did this to try and take over Christianity.

All the evidence show that the Mithras myth was a copycat of Jesus. The claims of the Atheists and Neo-Pagans that Jesus was a copycat of Mithras is not true - it was the other way round![39]

17-23 December: Saturnalia (Roman[40])

By the beginning of December the farmers finished their autumn planting. Saturn was now honoured with a festival to ensure a good harvest. Apparently his name is derived from the Latin word "satus" (past participle of the word "to sow").

Originally it was a one day celebration on 17 December. Later on it was celebrated for a whole week.

They gave each other presents, especially candles (The lit candles symbolized the return of the sun). The trees were decorated with sun and star symbols and ornaments that represented deities.

Those who could afford it sacrificed a suckling pig to Saturn. They had gladiator fights in the circuses. At the end of the feast their dead bodies were given as a sacrifice to Saturn.

Saturnalia was the biggest and wildest party of year, done on a national scale. Slaves were treated as equals and didn't work. People wore colourful clothes in public and "liberty caps"[41] to symbolize the freedom of the season.

People got drunk, sang nude on the streets, took part in orgies etcetera. Misbehaviour was encouraged. They appointed a Lord of Misrule to rule for this week and to organise festival events.

---

[39] Sources: Mithra vs Jesus [http://tektonics.org/copycat/mithra.php] and http://coldcasechristianity.com/2014/is-jesus-simply-a-retelling-of-the-mithras-mythology

[40] Up until 46 BC the Romans had a lunisolar calendar, so their feasts dates were not on the same time each year according to our solar Gregorian calendar. Their calculation for the winter solstice was also a day late, because they waited for it to be visible.

[41] It is also called a Pileus, Freedman, Phrygian, Mithras and Santa's Cap.

21/22 December: Yule (European)

Yule[42] refers to the time around the winter solstice. One of Odin's many names was Jólnir (master of Yule). This was the time for the flying Wild Hunt. The prey would often be a wild boar[43]. Odin (Woden) was the leader of the hunting party. This hunt was associated with the change of seasons. Yule was also a festival to celebrate the annual rebirth of the Celtic sun god Lugh.

It was a time for feasting and merrymaking. Fresh meat was plentiful because people slaughtered a lot of livestock so that they wouldn't have to be fed during the winter. They drank lots of beer and made toasts to the gods and to their king.

Candles were lit[44] and a big *yule log* was burned to celebrate the return of the sun by lighting up the place. In Germany a tree was set ablaze and people danced around it.

Druids harvested mistletoe under a waxing moon, which were fed to animals to guarantee their fertility. They sacrificed 2 white bulls as part of the ritual[45]. Mistletoe is associated with Frigga, the goddess of sex, fertility and love (That is why people kiss under it).

The round evergreen wreath is a reminder that life still remains in the darkness of winter. It is made round to symbolize the Sun and the circle of life (It could also symbolize the female genitals, like the flower wreath used during Beltane).

---

[42] There has been a revival of pagan religions since the 1960's, a very clear sign of the dawning of the Age of Aquarius.

(When I write in past tense it is to indicate historical events, but it is difficult to make the distinction. For example, Saturnalia is not really celebrated today as a feast, but many of its customs have been incorporated into Yule and "Christmas" celebrations.)

[43] Christmas ham or gammon is a commemoration of Odin's wild boar hunt and the suckling pig that was offered to Saturnus during Saturnalia.

[44] The Dutch word for Christmas is "Kersfees", *candle feast*.

[45] Maybe there is a connection with Mithras who killed the white cosmic bull?

23 December (winter solstice): Feast of Sokar[46] (Egyptian)

Osiris was married to his sister Isis. His enemies trapped him inside a chest and killed him. They threw the chest into a river. Isis went looking for the chest and found it at a place called Byblus[47]. Eventually she retrieved it (The king of Byblus used it as a pillar for the roof of his house or palace). When she opened the chest and saw the face of Osiris she wept bitterly.

She took the chest back with her to Egypt. She hid the chest and went to visit her son (the first Horus) in the city Butosus. While she was away his enemies found the chest. They cut his body into 14 pieces and scattered it. Isis found all the pieces except his penis. She created one for him and consecrated it. The Egyptians hold a festival in honour of the phallus that Isis created[48].

She reassembled him. She brought him momentarily back to life with her love and grief and some magic spells, just long enough to have intercourse with him to get pregnant. At the following year's winter solstice (more probably the vernal equinox in the year after that[49]) Horus was born as Harpokrates (Horus the Child). She claimed that he was the reincarnation of Osiris.

---

[46] This version of the myth of the death of Osiris and his "reincarnation" as his son Horus is according to the historian Plutarch (c.46 Ad to c.120 AD).
"On Isis and Osiris". Plutarch's Morals: Theosophical Essays, tr. by Charles William King, [1908]
[http://www.sacred-texts.com/cla/plu/pte/pte04.htm] p. 11-16

[47] The king of Byblus was Melqart (Tammuz). His queen was Astarte (Asherah/ Ishtar).

[48] This festival is called "Raising of the Djed".
[https://www.ancient.eu/Djed/], [https://ancientegypt.hypermart.net/treeoflife/]

[49] Plutarch (pp. 11-56): Osiris was killed in the middle of November. Isis found his corps and he was mummified. The feast of his "rising" was on 23 December that year. Then there were some battles between Horus her son and Typhon. After that Isis got pregnant, in the 1st week of October. Her child was born premature. It could not have been that winter solstice, it had to be at the vernal equinox of the next year.

Isis convinced her followers that she was impregnated by Osiris's mummy, that Horus was born at the winter solstice, and then also at the vernal equinox. She must have been an extremely good liar, or her followers believed her because they didn't want to get killed.

Two events were celebrated at The Feast of Sokar:

- The rising of Osiris and
- The reincarnation of Osiris / birth of "Horus the child"

The "rising" refers to Osiris rising as an "august spirit" to take his place in the sky as king of the dead. (He was not resurrected.)

After his death Osiris merged into the triune god[50] Ptah-Sokar-Osiris. The Egyptians believed that the sun went through the underworld at night and was reborn in the morning.

Ptah-Sokar-Osiris, king of the underworld and god of reincarnation, was seen as the sun during the night. The sun was reborn every morning as Horus/Sokar. Sokar is a syncretized form of both Osiris and Horus. He is Osiris, and he is also his son Horus who is his reincarnation. Osiris is present at the birth of his son Horus/Sokar during the winter solstice.

A series of rituals and processions were performed from 8 to 26 December. They were enactments of the events that resulted in the death and rising of Osiris. One of the events was a funeral processions with the coffin of Osiris. It was intended to be more of an encouragement for people to make use of the present and to enjoy it[51], than a reminder to mourn for Osiris.

People made hollow boxes in the shape of the god Osiris, which were filled with Nile mud and planted with corn. The boxes were then wrapped like mummies and placed in a tomb. It was called an "Osiris Bed". The corn was expected to sprout as a symbol of the reincarnation of Osiris. Egyptians also placed fruitcakes in the tombs of loved ones to provide food for the afterlife.

The birth of Horus the son of Osiris was celebrated on the same day. An image of an infant Horus represented the new-born sun. On his birthday it was laid in a manger, and a statue of Isis was placed beside it. It was brought from the shrine and shown to the people.

---

[50] "Triune gods" or "triple deities" are found in many religions.
[51] Tomorrow their lives are over and they will be in coffins.

23 (25?[52]) December: Kikellia - Birth of Horus (Egyptian)

Another birthday celebration for Horus. In this midwinter solstice festival the virgin Kore gave birth to Aion. Kore is the hellenized transformation of Isis. Aion is identified with Dionysus, the Greek counterpart of Horus and Tammuz.

There was a large temple at Alexandria which was the shrine of Kore. On the eve before Kikellia people stayed up all night at her shrine. They sang hymns to her idol with flute accompaniment. The next morning torchbearers went down into an underground shrine.

They came up with a stretcher with a wooden image sitting on it. There were sign of the cross gold inlays on the image. The images was carried 7 times round the shrine. The people sang hymns and played flutes and tambourines.

They had a feast and then they took back the image into the underground shrine. The meaning of the ceremony was that the "virgin" Kore (Isis) gave birth to Aion (Horus).

Spring / Vernal Equinox festivals:

21 March : Feast of Shamo ("Egyptian Easter")

Horus was born as the Eternal Son[53] on the vernal equinox. The Feast of Shamo[54] ("renewal of life"), an ancient harvest festival, was celebrated on that day. It marked the beginning of spring.

Not only crops but also fish were harvested. (As the flood waters of the Nile receded fish were trapped in shallow pools.)

---

[52] Some 25 December dates fall on 23 December on our Gregorian calendar. See *Appendix E : The "Jesus myth" hoax* on page 142.

[53] "On Isis and Osiris". Plutarch's Morals: Theosophical Essays, tr. by Charles William King, [1908]. p.56

[54] Main sources: https://www.officeholidays.com/countries/egypt/sham_el_nessim.php] and [http://cairoscene.com/ArtsAndCulture/Sham-El-Nessim-s-Roots-in-Ancient-Egypt]

They ate salted fish[55], lettuce, and onions, and also offered it to their deities. People hung onions in their doorways to keep away evil spirits. Or they placed them under their children's pillows that night to summon the god Sokar (Osiris[56]).

They also ate chickpeas and eggs. Eggs were dyed and hung in temples as symbols of regeneration. People wrote their wishes on these eggs. They put them in baskets which they hung on trees or the roofs of their houses. They were hoping that their deities would grant them their wishes by dawn.

Before dawn people went to the meadows and gardens[57] or the banks of the Nile to watch the sunrise. They took food and flowers with them and had a picnic.

The name of the festival changed to "shamm" (smelling and breathing) during the Coptic period[58], and the word "nessim" (breeze) was added.

It is now called Sham El-Nissem, which means "inhaling the breeze". The feast was also moved from the date of the vernal equinox to the Monday after the Coptic Easter[59].

Today Sham El-Nessim is celebrated outside with picnics. People are encouraged to spend some time outside and "smell the breeze" (breath in some fresh air). People eat fish, green onions, termis (lupin seeds) and boiled painted eggs. (Some "breezes" probably smell better outside …)

---

[55] Maybe the origin of the "gefilte fish" of the Jews? (It is a traditional dish that Jews eat during Passover).

[56] Refai, Mohamed. (2016). Monograph on fungal diseases of fish Part 1. p.43

[57] The feast was called "Tshom Ni Sime" before it was called "Sham El-Nessim" ("tshom" means "gardens" and "ni sime" means "meadows".)

[58] 3rd to 7th century AD

[59] The Coptic Easter is celebrated on the Sunday after the first full moon that follows the vernal equinox.

20/21 March: Feast of Ishtar

Jer 7:18 The children gather wood, and the fathers kindle the fire, and the women knead their dough, to make cakes to the queen of heaven, and to pour out drink offerings unto other gods, that they may provoke me to anger.

Eze 8:14-16 Then he brought me to the door of the gate of Yahweh's house which was toward the north; and, behold, there sat women weeping for Tammuz. Then said he unto me: Hast thou seen this, O son of man? Thou shall see greater abominations than these. And he brought me into the inner court of Yahweh's house, and, behold, at the door of the temple of Yahweh, between the porch and the altar, were about twenty-five men, with their backs toward the temple of Yahweh, and their faces toward the east; and they worshipped the rising sun.

The Feast of Ishtar is the celebration of the return of Ishtar and the death of her husband Tammuz[60].

Ishtar[61] went to visit her sister Ereshkigal, the queen of the underworld. Ishtar dared to sit on her throne. The Anunnaki[62] immediately judged her and turned her into a corpse. Because she was the fertiliy goddess all sexual inercourse ceased, causing famine.

Ereshkigal was persuaded to let Ishtar go, but she allowed it only on the condition that she finds a substitute spirit to take her place in the underworld. Ishtar could not find any being who was not mourning her passing, until she got home.

She saw her husband Tammuz sitting on the throne. He was not in mourning.

---

[60] This version is the most common one and is backed by historical records. Online (11/2018): [http://www.newworldencyclopedia.org/entry/Tammuz]

[61] People believed that an enormous egg fell from heaven and miraculously hatched Ishtar. She is called Ashtoreth or Asherah in the Bible ("Astarte" in the LXX).

[62] 7 Judges before the throne of Ereshkigal, the ruler of the underworld. Some people believe that they are fallen angels or the spirits of their hybrid offspring the Nephilim (Gen 6:1-4, Num 13:33, 2 Pet 2:4).

Ishtar was furious and gave him over to he demons who escorted her. After a while Ishtar calmed down and softened her decree, restoring her husband Tammuz to life for a portion of the year. That was possible because his sister agreed to take his place in the underworld when he was among the living.

Tammuz dies every vernal equinox. People then lament his death. But because of his death Ishtar, the goddess of fertility, can reign, causing spring and new life.

Tammuz was the god of agriculture who regulated the seasons. He symbolized the annual cycle of vegetation.

A Baal offering table was found on an archaeological site in Hazor, Israel. It is described as follows: "a basalt offering table, pillar-shaped, with a carved symbol of the storm god Baal on its side. That symbol was a circle with a cross in the center"[63].

The equilateral cross within a circle is called a solar cross or a sun cross [64]. The crosses are also found on the small round Ishtar buns ("hot cross buns").

---

[63] University of Illinois, Religious Studies, Hazor.
Online (11/2018) from the archived page [http://web.archive.org/web/20040812103831/http://www.relst.uiuc.edu/Courses/106/LBpages/page15.html]

[64] It is probably the oldest religious symbol in the world. It represents the following: The sun deity and the 4 seasons. The 2 solstices and the 2 equinoxes. The 4 phases of the moon. Some witches wear it instead of the pentagram.

Feast of Ishtar celebrations

The Feast of Ishtar was a lunisolar festival: its date was determined by the vernal equinox and the new moon.

People made round buns for the Queen of Heaven to eat during the feast. The origins of "easter buns" goes back to about 1500 years BC. Ancient cultures offered small round buns to their goddesses on their spring festivals. It was on the first day of the full moon after the vernal equinox. The small round buns represented the sun.

At sunrise on Easter Sunday they celebrated the return of Ishtar. They mourned the death of Tammuz[65] and baked round raisin buns for his wife Ishtar, the Queen of Heaven.

Another easter goddess was Ostara (Eostre). She is depicted with a hare's head or hare's ears. Her consort was the sun god. Ostara was the Germanic goddess of the dawn. According to myth she changed a bird into an egg laying hare[66].

Hares symbolizes fertility and sex. The modern day version are bunnies. Hugh Hefner chose the rabbit for the logo of his sex magazine Playboy because it had a sexual meaning.

The "easter egg" is a pagan fertility symbol. The origin of the dyed eggs is the Feast of Shamo, which is a feast that celebrates the birth of Horus as the Eternal Son. The searching for the eggs probably comes from the Feast of Sokar, where people did an reenactment of the search for the body of Osiris.

---

[65] There is an old Mesopotamian clay tablet in the Louvre Museum in Paris dating to the Amorite Period (c. 2000-1600 BC), containing a lamentation over the death of Dumuzid (Tammuz).

[66] The association of the pagan celebration of spring with eggs are thus based on at least 3 myths: At the Egyptian Feast of Shamo eggs were dyed and used for fertility rites and good luck, Ishtar who was hatched from an egg, and the egg laying hare of Ostara.

It is true that infants were sacrificed to Tammuz/Baal/Moloch, but I could not find any evidence for the claim that it was part of the Feast of Ishtar celebrations. I also could not find any records that indicated that eggs were dipped in their blood and hidden away during Easter.

Similarities between the winter and spring festivals

1. The Feast of Kikelia reminds us of the Ishtar festival in spring: Aion is associated with the 4 seasons of the year and winter and summer, just like Tammuz. Images of Kore have crosses on them, which is the symbol of Tammuz. His resurrection is celebrated at the spring festival.

2. Osiris was the Sun and Isis the Moon, and they called the Moon the mother of Saturn. This links Saturnalia not only to Saturn, but to Horus as well. Saturn can be linked to the Feast of Ishtar as well, because he was a Roman god of agriculture, just like the Babylonian Tammuz.

3. Horus is born at the winter solstice as Horus the Child (Harpocrates). He is born at the vernal equinox as the adult Horus, the Eternal Son[67].

4. Isis (the main goddess of the winter solstice festivals) went to Byblos to recover the corpse of Osiris. She asked Astarte for the body. Astarte is also called Asherah and Ishtar, the main goddess of the spring festivals.

5. At the winter solstice relatives of the deceased offered onions to the deities. The onion protected the deceased and it was an instrument of a "solar rebirth". They put onions in front of the nostrils of the deceased to allow him to acquire the new breath of life. At the Egyptian spring festival Sham El-Nissem ("inhaling the breeze") people smell the onions.

6. The winter solstice festivals are about the days starting to getting longer after the shortest day. The spring equinox festivals are about the days getting longer than the night after they were of equal length.

7. During the Roman winter and spring festivals people got drunk and had wild parties and orgies.

8. Sacrifices were made to fertility and sun deities.

---

[67] We can probably use the analogy that the baby's head become visible on the winter solstice, with the final delivery on the vernal equinox. (The poor mother...)

The star of Remphan

In Egyption mythology the 5 point star represents the star Sirius, the bright star of Isis. In Egypt the new year began at the heliacal rising of Sirius. In ancient times this occured in early July after the solstice. It heralded the flooding of the Nile river (The Egyptians believed that the Nile flooded every year because Isis was crying over her Osiris, her dead husband). Later on it was also called the *dog star* (It represents the dog of Orion. He was a shepherd/hunter/ warrior).

Sirius is usually shown on the head of Isis. Isis was represented by the 8 pointed star. It also represents Ishtar (aka Inanna), the Queen of Heaven (Stellar Maris), the Maltese Cross, the Chaos Star (Freemasons) and the Wiccan Wheel of the Year used by Druids.

About 19 years ago archeologists found the Al-Hamra cube at Tayma, an ancient city in Saudi Arabia. The city was founded by Tayma, a son of Ismael, a son of Abraham (Gen 25:15, 1 Chr 1:30).

Tayma[68] was a very important stopping place for caravans traveling between Egypt and Mesopotamia, and to and from southern Arabia, because it is situated at an oasis in one of the driest places on earth.

The prophet Isaiah probably referred to Bir Hadaj, the largest and possibly the oldest working well in Saudi Arabia, which sits in the middle of Tayma:

> *Isa 21:13+14 The burden upon Arabia. In the forest in Arabia shall you lodge, O you travelling companies of Dedanim. The inhabitants of the land of Tayma brought water to him who was thirsty...*

The Israelites are descendants of another son of Abraham, Isaac. If the Israelites made a golden calf, then it seems logical that the star of Remphan could have been the 8 pointed one that represents Isis or Ishtar (which they also worshipped, Jeremiah chapter 44).

---

[68] Google Maps link: [https://goo.gl/maps/RTiEsCrwzwG2]

André-Salvini describes the Al- Hamra cube as follows:

a "thoroughly Babylonian" priest standing before an altar to the Egyptian bull-god Apis, set against a background of winged emblems and an eight-pointed star that is probably derived from Anatolian civilization.

"Despite borrowing imagery from other cultures, the art is totally unique," she explains. "It possesses a seminal Arabic identity that's neither Meso- potamian nor Egyptian nor Syrian."[69]

Left[70]: Stele dedicated to Isis and the Apis bull. Isis is shown behind Apis. The bull represents her husband Osiris.

---

[69] Richard Covington (2011) "Roads of Arabia" (pages 24-35 of the March/April 2011 print edition of *Saudi Aramco World*). Online (10/2018) [http://archive.aramcoworld.com/issue/201102/roads.of.arabia.htm]

[70] Image: Commons Wikimedia
Louvre_stele_portier_temple_Horoudja.JPG

Obelisks and trees, pillars and poles

Lev 26:1 You shall make yourselves no idols nor graven image, **neither rear you up a pillar**, *neither shall you set up any* **carved stone** *in your land, to bow down unto it: for I am Yahweh your God.*

Raising the Djed pillar[71]

Every year, a few days after the Feast of Sokar, the Egyptians hold a festival called "Raising the Djed". It was in honour of the phallus that Isis created for Osiris.

The Egyptians made huge stone obelisks. Apparently obelisks are very large Djed pillars[72]. According to some researchers the word 'obelisk' literally means 'Baal's shaft' or 'Baal's organ of reproduction'.

A similar erection, I mean "pole raising" event, is probably the Maypole dance on the Beltane feast. Beltane means "fire of Bel". Bel [73] is the Celtic sun god, the husband of the mother goddess.

The Maypole is a phallic fertility symbol. The ring of flowers at the top represents the fertility goddess and her genitals. Its origin was a "sacred tree", the so-called "Tree of Life".

---

[71] WC: Jon Bodsworth - Egypt Archive. (Image cropped by author)

[72] Many churches have steeples, which are just modified obelisks. (Some even have obelisks!). They are an abomination to God.

[73] This could be Nimrod, who was also called Bel.

The "asherim" and the "Tree of Life"

Deities were worshiped in the form of wooden poles (sometimes carved), sacred trees, carved tree trunks, carved wooden images and engraved stone images[74]. The Hebrew words to describe them are usually translated as "images" and "groves"[75]. It might be useful if we amplify the wording of the following verses a little bit, in context of what we know about Asherah and the context of the verses:

> Deu 7:5 But thus shall you deal with them: You shall destroy their altars, and break down their (stone) pillars/columns, and cut down their trees and (carved) poles (for Asherah), and burn their carved images with fire.

> Deu 12:3 And you shall overthrow their altars, and break their (stone) pillars/columns, and burn their trees and (carved) poles (for Asherah); and you shall hew down the carved (wooden) images of their gods, and destroy the names of them out of that place.

> 2 Chr 34:4 And they broke down the altars of the Baals in his presence. The (wooden) sun pillars/images which were placed on high above the altars he cut down. The standing stone columns/images of Asherah and the engraved (stone) images and the molten images he broke in pieces and made dust of them, and strewed it upon the graves of them that had sacrificed unto them.

> 1Ki 14:23 For they also built them high places, and (stone) pillars/columns, and (standing stone) columns/images of Asherah, on every high hill, and under every green tree.

The poles and pillars and trees usually represented phalluses, but often they represented female deities (especially Asherah / Ishtar).

---

[74] John Day (1986). "Asherah in the Hebrew Bible and Northwest Semitic Literature". *Journal of Biblical Literature*, Vol. 105, No. 3 (Sep., 1986)

[75] The following Hebrew words are usually translated as "images":
  H2553 - Chamman: sun pillar, sun image
  H4541 - Massekah: molten image
  H4676 - Matstsaybah: pillar, column, obelisk, stump of tree
  H6456 - Pesil: carved/graven/engraved image

Hathor the Egyptian tree goddess[76]

Ishtar is often depicted with the "Tree of Life".

She was equated with Hathor, who was a tree goddess also (the consort of Horus).

The Israelites used to go and have sex under "sacred" trees:

Isa 57:5 You worship idols with your lust under every green tree. You slay the children in the valleys, under the clifts of the rocks.

Jer 2:20b upon every high hill and under every green tree thou sprawled and prostituted thyself.

Jer 3:6b Israel... is gone up upon every high mountain and under every green tree, and there has committed fornication.

Some of the syncretistic pagans regarded Asherah as Yahweh's consort[77]. But God made it very clear that she is not his consort. There is only one Bride for Him: those who are in Covenant with Him.

Deu 16:21-22 Thou shalt not plant any tree that represents Asherah beside the altar of Yahweh thy God, which thou shall make thee. Neither shalt thou set thee up any pillars/ columns; which Yahweh thy God hates.

---

[76] Creative Commons original: Asaf Braverman (image is cropped) [https://creativecommons.org/licenses/by-nc-sa/2.0/]

[77] John Day (1986). "Asherah in the Hebrew Bible and Northwest Semitic Literature". *Journal of Biblical Literature*, Vol. 105, No. 3 (Sep., 1986), p. 392-393

Christian or pagan celebrations: Your choice

2 Kng 17:15 And they rejected his statutes, and his Covenant ... and went after the heathen that were round about them, concerning whom Yahweh had charged them, that they should not do like them.

Jer 10:2a Thus says Yahweh: Learn not the way of the heathen

1 Cor 10:14 Therefore, my dearly beloved, flee from idolatry.

Christian Christmas	Pagan Solstice celebrations
Suggestion: Lamb Jesus was the Lamb of God	"Christmas ham": Odin's hunt, suckling pig sacrificed to Saturn
Wise men bring gifts	Odin / Santa Claus brings gifts
Nativity scene	Tree and mistletoe
Songs about Jesus' birth	Songs about Santa and Yuletide
Watch Christian movies, read story of Jesus' birth	Watch Yule movies

Passover	Pagan Spring Equinox
Eat unleavened bread and bitter herbs in memory of Jesus.	Eat chocolate bunny in memory of Ostara and hot cross buns in memory of Ishtar and Tammuz.
Celebrate on 14 Aviv / Nissan as prescribed in the Bible	Celebrate first Sunday after full moon after equinox
Celebrate the Feast of the First Fruits[78] as prescribed in the Bible (wave a sheaf before the LORD)	Celebrate Ishtar Sunday with sunrise (Jesus had risen before sunrise)
Search for the Afikomen[79]	Search for bunny eggs

---

[78] Jesus rose on the Feast of the First Fruits. He was the first sheave that rose from the dead (Lev 23:11, John 12:24, 1 Cor 15:20-23).

[79] It means "The Coming One". It was a specific piece of bread that Jesus used for Communion at the Last Supper. (Download a free Messianic Passover celebration guide at [https://www.moadim.org.za/en/passoverfeast].)

The celestial bodies created for signs and seasons and times

Gen 1:14 And God (Elohim) said: Let there be lights in the firmament of the heaven to divide the day from the night; and let them be for signs, and for appointed times and seasons (moadim), and for days, and years.

Gen 1:16 And God (Elohim) made the two great lights: the greater light to rule the day, and the lesser light to rule the night; also the stars[80].

Psa 104:19 He appointed the moon for seasons: the sun knows his going down.

In the Pseudo-Jonathan Targum (an ancient Aramaic paraphrase) it says:

God said, "Let there be lights in the firmament of the heavens to separate the day from the night, and let them serve as signs and as festival times, and for counting the reckoning of days, and for sanctifying the beginnings of months and the beginnings of years, the intercalations of months and the intercalations of years, the solstices, the new moon, and the cycles (of the sun)."[81]

God planned everything from the beginning. When God created the celestial bodies He put them in orbits. He knows when and where there are conjunctions going to take place.

God also influenced the people who named the stars and planets and constellations. They attached to them certain symbolisms and meanings which were related to their appearance and behaviour. Without it they would not have messages for us.

1Cor 15:41 There is one glory of the sun, and another glory of the moon, and another glory of the stars: for one star differs from another star in glory.

---

[80] All celestial bodies, except the sun and moon, were called "stars" in ancient times.

[81] Michael Maher (1992), *Targum Pseudo-Jonathan Genesis: Translated, with Introduction and Notes* (The Aramaic Bible 1B; Collegeville: Liturgical Press)

The prophets used the same names that the astronomers and astrologers are still using. God also calls the stars and constellations by the names which were given by humans[82]:

Amos 5:8 Seek him who makes the seven stars and Orion ... Yahweh is his name

Job 9:9 Which makes Arcturus, Orion, and Pleiades, and the chambers of the south.

God says that He is the one who brings forth the zodiac constellations in their times. Biblical astronomical signs are usually referred to as the Mazzaroth (the Hebrew word for the constellations of the zodiac).

Their names and symbolism enabled the wise men to correctly interpret the signs at the birth of Jesus. There hasn't been anything similar for thousands of years either before or after the birth of Jesus Christ.

Psa 19:1 The heavens declare the glory of God; and the firmament showeth his handiwork.

Psa 148:3 Praise you him, sun and moon: praise him, all you stars of light.

When God told Moses to lead the Israelites out of Egypt on a certain predetermined date on a specific month there was a reason: since then that month was the first month of their year, and Passover would always be on the full moon in the middle of that month.

The same with the date of birth of Jesus. It had to happen on a specific date, otherwise there would be no star message in the heavens. God determined the exact date. The celestial bodies don't determine anything, they are just signs to inform us what is happening.

---

[82] Likewise Adam named the animals (Gen 2).

Venus and Jupiter conjunction: The "Star of Bethlehem"

Venus and Jupiter were two of the most important celestial bodies. From archeology we know that the Babylonians not only observed their positions and paths, but also calculated it beforehand.

The Venus tablet (tablet 63) is part of the Enuma Anu Enlil series of tablets.

They were created from information and observations done over centuries.

They were used to calculate astronomical events, which were used to make astrological predictions.

Image: WC (cropped)

They figured out how to calculate the area of a trapezoid (also called a trapezium, a mathematical shape in geometry). They used it to develop a technique to calculate the distance that Jupiter travelled (A similar technique was only re-invented in the 14th century AD!).

The Babylonians[83] had developed *"abstract mathematical, geometrical ideas about the connection between motion, position and time that are so common to any modern physicist or mathematician"*.

Very close visible conjunctions between Jupiter and Venus (seen as "one star"[84]) in two sequential years only happened three times the past 3000 years. And the only time that one of them was an occultation was in the year when Jesus was born.

This close conjunction of Venus and Jupiter is called the **Star of Bethlehem** by many astronomers, and with good reason!

---

[83] Mathieu Ossendrijver (2016): *"Ancient Babylonian astronomers calculated Jupiter's position from the area under a time-velocity graph"*, Science 351 (January 29, 2016), 482-484.

[84] The wise men called it "the same star" when they saw it the second time (when they went to visit Jesus in Bethlehem).

3 - 2 BC: The most amazing series of conjunctions ever

There was an amazing series of conjunctions that took place in 3 to 2 BC, that had never happened in the 2000 years before or after that time. It is so spectacular (in an astronomical sense) that many planetariums have revised their Christmas programs to correspond with dating theories and data of leading recognized authorities like Dr. Ernest Martin. His book, "The Star that Astonished the World," is considered the authoritative work on the date of Jesus's birth based upon astronomical events. More and more people are reconsidering the birth date of Jesus, and they reject the 4 BC date.

In their article "A Dazzling Duo" NASA describes the conjunction of 2 BC as a "dazzling point of light" that made history[85]. There has never been a brighter and closer conjunction of Venus and Jupiter for 2000 years before or since then. They were so near (just 6 arc seconds in astronomical terminology) that they seemed to merge into a single very bright star.

Susan S. Carroll says that 3-2 BC was "one of the most remarkable periods in terms of celestial events in the last 3000 years".[86]

Michael Magee, director of UA's Flaudrau Planetarium, says the following: "There are Chinese writings. There are Arab writing of the day that all contribute to the history of what was going on and researchers have lots of material to look over to confirm it all... Ancient records actually mention a bright star in the east in August of 3 BC."[87]

Robert McIvor spent three decades researching this subject. He cites ancient Chinese and Korean star records, paintings in Roman catacombs and coins from various countries which refer to an unusual new star about the time of Jesus' birth.[88]

---

[85] [https://science.nasa.gov/science-news/science-at-nasa/2002/24may_duo/]

[86] S. Carroll (1997). The Star of Bethlehem: An Astronomical and Historical Perspective

[87] Source: KGUN9-TV, December 2016: Astronomers' theory of the Star of Bethlehem [http://www.kgun9.com/news/local-news/astronomers-theory-of-the-star-of-bethlehem]

[88] Robert McIvor (1998). *Star of Bethlehem Star of Messiah*. (Overland Press)

The two bright stars that proclaimed the birth of Jesus

There is a legal principle in the Bible that there must be at least two witnesses in order to establish a matter:

> Deu 19:15b *at the mouth of two witnesses, or at the mouth of three witnesses, shall the matter be established.*

> 2Co 13:1b *In the mouth of two or three witnesses shall every word be established.*

From an astronomical perspective the following verse can also refer to stars:

> Rev 22:16 *I Yeshua have sent mine angel to testify unto you these things in the assemblies. I am the root and the offspring (Tsemech) of David, and the bright and morning star (close conjunction of Venus and Jupiter).*

The Star of Bethlehem: The Righteous Bright Morning Star

Venus is called the bright morning star[89]. It is a very bright star (it can sometimes even be seen during the day!).

In Isa 14:12 the prophet Isaiah refers to king Nebuchadnezzar of Babylon as "heylel ben shachar", the *bright or shining*[90] *son of the dawn*. He compares his coming downfall to the star Venus falling from the sky.

The Star of Bethlehem is the conjunction of Venus and Jupiter. The Hebrew name for Jupiter is Tzadik and it means "Righteous".

So when you see Venus and Jupiter together as if they are one (as in 3 BC and 2 BC) near the star Regulus (the King star) in the constellation Leo (Lion of Judah), then in Hebrew it could have the meaning of **The Righteous Bright Morning Star.**

---

[89] Planets and very close conjunctions were called stars in ancient times.

[90] In some Bibles it is translated as Lucifer, but nowhere in Scripture is Satan called Lucifer.

The Star of the Messiah: The Branch in the hand of the Virgin

Tsemech is one of the brightest stars (the 16th brightest star in the entire sky). Hindu observers called it Citrā, meaning "bright." Its ancient Hebrew name is *Tsemech*.

"The brightest star in Virgo has an ancient name handed down to us in all the star maps, in which the hebrew word (nnצ) **Tsemech** is preserved. It is called in Arabic Al Zimach, which means the branch. This star is the ear of corn which she holds in her left hand. Hence the star has a modern Latin name, which has almost superseded the ancient one, Spica, which means, an ear of corn.

But this hides the great truth revealed by its name *Al Zimach*. It foretold the coming of him who should bear this name. The same Divine inspiration has, in the written Word, four times connected it with him. There are twenty Hebrew words translated "Branch," but only one of them (Tsemech) is used exclusively of the Messiah and this word only four times."[91]

> *Jer 23:5 Behold, the days come, says Yahweh, that I will raise unto David a **Righteous Branch**, and he shall reign as King and prosper, and shall execute judgment and justice in the earth.*

> *Jer 33:15 In those days, and at that time, will I cause **The Branch** of righteousness to grow up unto David; and he shall execute judgment and righteousness in the land*

> *Zec 3:8 Hear now, O Joshua the high priest, thou, and thy fellows that sit before thee: for they are men wondered at: for, behold, I will bring forth my servant **The Branch**.*

> *Zec 6:12 And speak unto him, saying: Thus speaks Yahweh of hosts, saying: Behold the man whose name is **Branch**; and he shall grow up out of his place, and he shall build the Temple of Yahweh.*

---

[91] E.W. Bullinger (1893). *The Witness of the Stars*
(Kregel Publications, 2000, pp.31-21. Reprint of the 1893 Edition)

The importance of the Vernal Equinox and Tsemech

The Biblical year starts at the new moon after the vernal equinox. The Sages base their ruling that Pesach must always be in spring, i.o.w after the vernal equinox, on the following verse:

Deu 16:1 Observe the month of Aviv, and keep the passover unto Yahweh thy God; for in the month of Aviv Yahweh thy God brought thee forth out of Egypt by night.

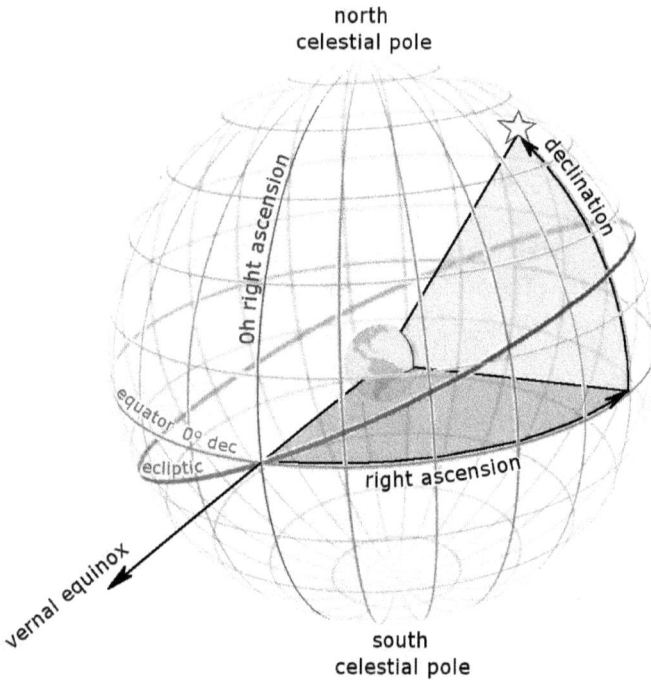

WC: Right ascension & declination on celestial sphere. The Vernal Equinox is the point of reference to indicate the position of stars in astronomy.

According to the Dead Sea Scrolls the Essenes started their calendar on or after the vernal equinox (usually within a week).

Philo, the Jewish historian and contemporary of Jesus and his disciples, wrote that Moses established the moon of the vernal equinox as the beginning of the first month of the year[92].

---

[92] *The Works of Philo*, On the Life of Moses II, chapter XLI, Prt 222 & 224

Tsemech, the spring star of the barley harvest

Tsemech is associated with the sowing and harvesting of barley. Barley was the first grain that was sown after the heliacal setting of Tsemech on 31 August, usually after the first rains. Tsemech also proclaimed the coming of spring and the time to harvest the barley. Its Latin name Spica comes from the Latin *spica virginis*, which means "Virgo's ear of grain".

The virgin of the *Virgo constellation* has a stalk of barley (the star Tsemech) in her hand, representative of the harvest to come. In some cultures she was called the "Wheat-Bearing Maiden".

A number of pagan temples were oriented to Tsemech's setting in the west. Their year began in autumn.

The Biblical year begins in spring, after the vernal equinox. Tsemech was visible the entire night during the month of March. The ancient Chinese considered Tsemech as a special **star of spring** and called it *Kio*, the horn.[93]

> *Luk 1:68+69 Blessed be Yahweh God of Israel; for he has visited and redeemed his people, and has raised up an horn of salvation for us in the house of his servant David*

The Temple in Jerusalem were oriented to the east, facing Tsemech whenever it rose. During the reign of Herod the Great, the last Jewish king, up to the destruction of the Second Temple in 70 AD, the star Tsemech rose exactly in the east and set exactly in the west.[94]

The Hebrew word for spring is *aviv* and it refers to something that is green, tender or young - like the sheaf of barley in the hand of Virgo. The Hebrew word for barley is also *aviv.*

Aviv is also the Biblical name for the first month after the vernal equinox, the first month of the religious year.

Jesus was the grain that had to die - John 12:24

---

[93] http://www.constellation-guide.com/spica/

[94] The positions where stars rise and set is not stationary, it changes slowly because of the "wobbling" of the axis of the earth.

Part 3: Calculating the date of birth of Jesus

Calendars and the traditional dates of birth of Jesus

The year of the traditional date of birth for Jesus was in 2 BC. Ancient writers gave the dates as follows:

	Writers	Date[95]	Year	Month
1.	Lucas	70 CE	2 BC	(not in winter)
2.	Clement[96]	195 CE	2 BC	11 Tubi (6 January)
3.	Irenaeus	180 CE	2 BC	-
4.	Tertullian	200 CE	2 BC	6 January
5.	Hippolytus	210 CE	2 BC	2 April / Passover
6.	Sextus	221 CE	2 BC	25 December
7.	Origen	231 CE	2 BC	-
8.	Cyprian	243 CE	-	28 March
9.	Eusebius	340 CE	2 BC	-
10.	Epiphanius	357 CE	2 BC	6 January
11.	Apollinaris	370 CE	2 BC	January
12.	Orosius	418 CE	2 BC	-

Conclusion:
Ancient writers agreed that Jesus was born in 2 BC[97]

---

[95] The date column refers to the approximate date of the source.

[96] Clement also mentions some non-prevalent dates for the day and month. (He used Egyption months.) One of them is 25 Pharmuthi (20 April,) which seems to be related to the 25 March date.

[97] See Appendix C on page 136 for details.

Similar articles that also prove that Jesus was born in 2 BC:

David W. Beyer (1998). *Josephus Reexamined: Unraveling the Twenty-Second Year of Tiberius*. Chronos, Kairos, Christos II, p.85-96

Allan Johnson (2013). *Rediscovering an ancient chronology*. Online (9/2018): [https://snofriacus.wordpress.com/studies/rediscovering-an-ancient-chronology/]

The 4 prevalent traditional dates of birth (day and month)

According to an ancient Jewish tradition, truly set-apart (holy and pious) people die on the same day that they are born. Therefore people believed that Jesus was born on Passover.

There is a tradition that the world was created on 25th March. They believed that Jesus was born on that date. This gave rise to the *original* traditional date of 25th March for the date of birth of Jesus. But Pesach did not fall on 25th March that year (nor for the previous 14 years).

Cyprian also believed that the world was created on 25 March, but he believed that Jesus was born on the 4th day of creation (28 March), the day that the sun was created. (He is called the "Sun of Righteousness".)

There were 4 different calendars in use which played a role in the establishment of the ancient traditional dates of birth for Jesus: Julian (Roman), Hebrew, ancient Greek (Macedonian) and Egyptian. If everybody followed the Roman calendar then 25th March and 25th December would have been the only 2 prevailing dates (other dates were the views of minorities).

The 6 January tradition comes from the Greek Orthodox scholars who used the ancient Greek calendar. Instead of 14th Aviv on the Hebrew calendar (for Pesach), they used the 14th day of the first spring month (Artemisios), which falls on 6 April. Nine months later comes to 6 January. There is a tradition that Jesus was born and baptized on the same day and that it was on 6 January. Some Eastern Orthodox churches still celebrate it on that date in Jerusalem as the "Feast of Epiphany" or "Feast of the Three Kings" (referring to the manifestation of the Messiah to the Gentiles as represented by the "wise men").

In the eastern Roman Empire (aka Byzantine Empire) the date of conception was considered to be the beginning of your life and it was more important than your date of birth, which is why they believed that Jesus was conceived on Pesach and born nine months later on 25 December.

The reason for the confusion between the dates for conception and birth is the choice of words of the ancient writers and the way that they were interpreted: Words like "genesis" and "epiphany" were interpreted as either conception or birth by different cultures.

That is how it happened that there were 4 prevailing traditional dates for the birth of Jesus: 25 March, 6 April, 25 December and 6 January.

Summary: Why there were 4 dates for the birth of Jesus:

1. 25 March was the original traditional date for the birth and death of Jesus.
2. Others saw the date not for his birth, but his conception. As a result we get the date of 25 December 9 months later.
3. The Greek (instead of the Hebrew) calendar was used to determine Pesach. The date of birth on 6 April was the result.
4. This date was also considered by some to be the date of conception. The date of 6 January was the result.

Herod the Great and the coming of Shiloh

Gen 49:10 The sceptre shall not depart from Judah, nor the ruler's staff from between his feet, until Shiloh come; and unto him shall the gathering of the people be.

Eze 37:19 Say unto them, Thus says Adonai Yahweh: Behold, I will take the stick of Joseph, which is in the hand of Ephraim, and the tribes of Israel his companions, and will put them with him, even with the stick of Judah, and make them one stick, and they shall be one in mine hand.

Eze 37:22 And I will make them one nation in the land upon the mountains of Israel; and one king shall be king to them all: and they shall be no more two nations, neither shall they be divided into two kingdoms any more at all.

Hos 1:11 Then shall the children of Judah and the children of Israel be gathered together[98], and appoint themselves one head[99], and they shall come up out of the land: for great shall be the day of Jezreel.

After the return of the exiles from Babylon there was one kingdom. All the Israelites who returned to Israel were joined unto Judah, just as was prophesied.[100]

During the Hasmonean reign the whole land was called Judea. Judaism was the official state religion. The king was also high priest.

Herod the Great killed the last Hasmonean king in 36 BC.

Shiloh (The Messiah) came when Jesus was born as the King of the Jews. The sceptre departed from Judah when Herod the Great died. He died in the same Biblical year that Jesus was born.

After the death of Herod the land of Israel was divided. The Sanhedrin still had some power but after the destruction of the Temple in 70 AD it also came to an end.

---

[98] Israelites from all tribes were exiled from Judah to Babylon. Since then there was no distinction made between Israelites of the different tribes, they were all known as Jews.

[99] The only time that Israel and Judah had rulers again over one united kingdom (after the exile to Babylon), was during the Hasmonean reign (135 BC to 37 BC). This prophecy does not point towards the Messiah, because he will not be appointed by anybody when he returns to reign as King of kings.

[100] Prophecies are very often fulfilled in a series of partial fulfilments, before the ultimate and final fulfilment. The Israelites did come back to Israel, but they were scattered again in 136 AD.

There are still some Jewish groups and individuals who are "making aliyah" (returning to Israel). This process will only be completed after the return of their Messiah, Yeshua HaMashiach (Jesus Christ).

The reign of Herod the Great

Herod the Great[101] reigned for 37 years, of which 34 years were after the death of Antigonus.[102] When we look at the regnal years of ancient kings, we need to be aware of the following facts:

1. Dates of their nominations (which can be compared with the anointing of Jewish kings), coronations, official and actual reign often are not the same.[103]

2. Some historians refer to the years that rulers ruled alone, others include coalitions. Backdating years of reign also was not uncommon.

3. Regnal years for Jewish kings are calculated from 1 Aviv (Nissan)[104], which is in March or April. It is necessary to take this into consideration,, because their regnal years always end after the end of Gregorian years (which ends in December).

According to Josephus Herod "received the kingdom" in 40 BC.[105] But Appian of Alexandria says that he became king in 39 BC.[106] Apparently the Roman Senate nominated him to be king of the Jews in 40 BC, and officially proclaimed him to be king in 39 BC.

But he could not reign yet, because Judea was under Parthian rule and they officially proclaimed Antigonus II Mattathias[107] as king in 40 BC. Herod first had to, with the aid of the Roman army, wage a war against Judea and conquer them before he could reign as king.

---

[101] Herod was called "the Great" because he built great monuments and he was the father of the Herodian dynasty. He is not to be confused with Herod the tetrarch who beheaded John the Baptist.

[102] Josephus, F (c.94 CE). *Jewish Antiquities 17.8.1 / XVII:191,*
Josephus, F (*c.75 CE.*) *The Jewish War 1.33.8,*)

[103] A good example of these different dates is the way that Saul became king of Israel – 1 Sam 10-11.

[104] Roland de Vaux (1973), *Ancient Israel Its Life and Institutions,* (Darton, Longman & Todd Ltd, London), 192-193. (See also 2 Chronicles 29:3+17, 30:2).

[105] Josephus, F (*Jewish Antiquities 14.5 / XIV:389*)

[106] Appian (*Civil Wars, 5.8.75*)

[107] He was the last Hasmonean priest king of Judea, he was both king and high priest.

Jerusalem was captured in July 37 BC and Antigonus II Mattathias was killed in the beginning of 36 BC[108] (Herod handed him over to the Romans who beheaded him).

Herod minted his first coin in 36 BC and dated it year 3, which confirms that his official reign started in 39 BC. His actual reign as king of Judea thus only began in 36 BC, which is why Josephus says that "from the days of Herod" to the destruction of the Temple in August 70 CE was 107 years.[109]

Consequently the end of his 37th year of official reign as king of Judea and the end of 34 regnal years after the death of Antigonus would be on 22 March (29 Adar) 1 BC.

Conclusion:
The 37th regnal year of Herod the Great was
from 5 April (1 Aviv[110]) 2 BC to 22 March (29 Adar) 1 BC.

The mistakes of the 4 BC date

One reason for the incorrect date of 4 BC for the death of Herod is probably because his regnal years are not taken into account.

The other reason is because they use a calendar that is based on the fixed 19-year metonic cycle, instead of fixing the intercalary months by the actual vernal equinox dates. The consequence of this mistake is that they choose the wrong year for the lunar eclipse to fix the date of Herod's death.

The fixed calendar was only used since 358 CE. Before that the high priest had to validate observations to fix intercalary months, which were added when it was deemed necessary.

---

[108] Titus Flavius Josephus (37 - 100 CE) states that Herod ended the Hasmonean era (which started 126 years earlier in 162 BC): -162 +126 = -36 *Jewish Antiquities 14.16.4 / XIV:490*

[109] *Jewish Antiquities 20.10.1 / XX:250*: 70 – 107 +1 (no year zero) = -36

[110] According to Jewish lunisolar calendar based on the vernal equinox dates

The date of Herod's death: A feast day after a lunar eclipse

A feast day

Herod died after an eclipse of the moon[111] that was after a day that the Jews observed as a fast, and before the Passover.[112] In the *Megillat Ta'anit* ("Roll of fasts") there are two feast dates on which there is no fasting: 2 Shevat and 7 Kislev. One celebrates the death of Herod[113], and the other one the death of King Alexander Jannaeus.

But there is no consensus between scholars about which date is for who, so we will consider both as possible dates. One of these two feast days, the one that falls between a lunar eclipse and Pesach in the final regnal year of Herod, is the day that he died.

The month Aviv is the first month of the Jewish year. It starts after the month of Adar in a normal year of 12 months, or after VeAdar (Adar II) in a Hebrew leap year (aka intercalary year). According to NASA's calculations the vernal equinox for 2 BC was on 21st March. Fixed calendars[114] give this date as 16 Aviv/Nissan.

Obviously it is a mistake, because **Pesach (14 Aviv/Nissan) must ALWAYS occur on or after the spring/vernal equinox**. If calculations showed that it will occur before the equinox then a second month of Adar was added to that year.

If we correct the fixed calendar[115] by moving VeAdar from 1 BC to 2 BC, then 7 Kislev falls on 4 December 2 BC and 2 Shevat falls on 28 January 1 BC.[116]

---

[111] *Antiquities 17.6.4 / XVII:166-167;*

[112] *Antiquities 17.9.3 / XVII:214, The Jewish War 2.1.3.*

[113] Herod the Great was very cruel and even predicted before his death that the Jews would celebrate his death with a festival - The Jewish War 1.33.6

[114] Fixed calendars are based on a fixed 19-year metonic cycle, where years 3, 6, 8, 11, 14, 17 and 19 are embolismic (leap years).

[115] According to the vernal equinox, as required by Jewish law.

[116] Hebrew dates are calculated according to the system that the Sanhedrin used at the time of Jesus. See footnotes on page 88 for details. [http://astropixels.com/ephemeris/phasescat/phases-0099.html]

(Fixed calendars use a fixed pattern. They might give a different date which would most probably be incorrect.)

The lunar eclipse

There were 2 lunar eclipses in the final regnal year of Herod: A partial eclipse on 17 July 2 BC, and a total eclipse on 10 January 1 BC.[117] The one on 17 July was followed by the Feast of Trumpets, not Pesach, so we can eliminate that one.

The lunar eclipse on 10 January 1 BC was only 5 days after the Fast of 10 Tevet on 5 January, and it is followed by Pesach. It was a total lunar eclipse, something which is rare. The following chronology perfectly fits all the historical evidence related to the death of Herod the Great:

> 5 January: The fast of 10 Tevet
>
> 10 January: Lunar eclipse (15 Tevet)
>
> 28 January: Feast date 2 Shevat = Death of Herod
>
> 17 April: Pesach on 14 Aviv (Nissan)

Conclusion:

Herod died on 28 January 1 BC.

This confirms Jesus' birth in 2 BC.

The priestly course of Abijah

Lucas gives us a chronological account for the birth of Jesus (Luke 1), starting with the priestly course of Abijah:

1. During the week of the priestly course of Abijah the angel Gabriel appeared to Zachariah. He told him that he will have a son which he must call John (Heb: Yochanan) (v5, 11-13).
2. As soon as his week was finished he went home (v23).
3. His wife conceived, hid herself for 5 months (v24).

---

[117] "Catalog of Lunar Eclipses: -0099 to 0000 (100 BC to 1 BC)", NASA, [https://eclipse.gsfc.nasa.gov/LEcat5/LE-0099-0000.html]

The two eclipses in 4 BC were only partial, and they also cannot be synchronized with all the other events.

4. The next day (the first day of the 6th month) the angel Gabriel visited Mary. He told her that she was going to give birth to the Messiah, and she conceived (v26-35).

5. Immediately Miryam went to visit Elizabeth (v39).

6. She was already pregnant when Elizabeth greeted her (v40-45).

7. Miryam stayed there for 3 months and then went to her own home (v56).

8. About a month later Elizabeth gave birth to Yochanan (v57).

Yochanan was conceived at the end of the priestly course of Abijah, and Jesus was conceived when Elizabeth was pregnant with Yochanan for 5 months.

We can therefore use the end dates of the weekly priestly Temple service to very accurately calculate the 2 possible dates of birth for Jesus.

The 24 week cycle of priestly courses

There were 24 priestly courses which followed a cycle of 24 weeks (1 Chr 24:7-18). The priests of each course officiated for a week, starting from one Sabbath to the next Sabbath (1 Chr 9:25, 2 Chr 23:8). This is confirmed by the Jewish historian Josephus[118].

This cycle of 24 weeks would continuously repeat itself. Rabbi Ari Shvat says the following[119]: "The Talmud (Erchin 11b; Y'rushalmi Shkalim 5, 3) and most commentaries and halachic codifiers state simply that the order of the 24 kohanic families would continuously repeat itself".

According to the Mishnah ('Arakin 11b and Ta'anith 29a) the course of Jehoiarib was on duty on the evening of the 9th of Av when the Temple was destroyed. That was on August 4, 70 CE.

---

[118] *Jewish Antiquities VII:365-366*

[119] Rabbi Ari Shvat. *Priestly courses (mishmarot hakehuna): cycles and leap years.* (Yeshiva Arutz Sheva)

Calendar Document B (4Q321)

On the Mishmarot Calendar of the Qumran scrolls (4Q320 and 4Q321, dated 50-25 BC) the courses of the priests are continuous.

Their 7-year sabbatical cycle started on the first Wednesday after the spring equinox during the course of Gamul. In 42 BC the cycle started on 25 March. This is in sync with the course of Jehoirarib in 70 CE.[120]

Therefore we know that the cycle of courses was not interrupted from at least 42 BC through to 70 CE. By counting backwards or forwards from one of the 2 known dates we can determine when Zachariah was on duty.

The dates of the priestly course of Abijah

There are more than 48 weeks in a year, so there would be at least 2 annual courses when the priests would have served at the Temple. By calculating backwards from the year of birth (2 BC), we can establish the time frame during which the courses of Abijah must have served when Zachariah was on duty.

---

[120] [http://www.johnpratt.com/items/docs/lds/meridian/2003/qumran.html#fn20]

When we add the 5 months of Elizabeth's pregnancy[121] to the 9½ months of Miryam's pregnancy,[122] then we get 14½ months from the time that the angel Gabriel appeared to Zachariah until the birth of Jesus.

We know that Jesus was born in 2 BC. If Jesus was born on 1 January, then the earliest date for the end of Zachariah's priestly course would be 14½ months earlier, i.e. 16 October 4 BC. If Jesus was born on 31 December, then the latest date would be 14½ months earlier, i.e. 15 October 3 BC.

Abijah served twice at the Temple in the period from 16 October 4 BC to 15 October 3 BC. The end dates of his priestly courses were 25 January 3 BC and 12 July 3 BC.

Calculating the possible dates of birth of Jesus

Calculations based on the 25 January 3 BC date:

Zachariah went home - conception of Elizabeth:	8 Shevat / 25 January 3 BC
5 Hebrew months later[123]:	8 Tammuz / 22 June 3 BC
Angelic visitation and conception of Miryam:	9 Tammuz / 23 June 3 BC
Birth 286 days later:	**1 Aviv / 5 April 2 BC**

---

[121] It was the day after Elizabeth was already 5 months pregnant when the angel Gabriel appeared to Miryam (Luk 1:24-26).

[122] According to Epiphanius the pregnancy of Miryam was "ten months less fourteen days and eight hours". This is apparently based on the apocryphal book "Wisdom of Solomon" (Wisdom 7:2). He was a Greek monk from Egypt and would have used Egyptian months (like Clement did). Egyptian months had 30 days: 10 x 30 – 14 = 286

The Panarion of Epiphanius of Salamis. Books II and III, translated by Frank Williams. — Second, revised edition (2011). p.61 (29.6)

Online (10/2018): [http://preteristarchive.com/Books/pdf/2013_williams_the-panarion-of-epiphanius-of-salamis_02-03.pdf]

[123] Biblical dates are almost always based on Jewish calendar.

Calculations using the 12 July 3 BC date:

Zachariah went home - conception of Elizabeth:	28 Tammuz / 12 July 3 BC
Five Hebrew months later:	28 Kislev / 6 December 3 BC
Angelic visitation and conception of Miryam:	29 Kislev / 7 December 3 BC
Birth 286 days later:	**20 Elul / 19 Sept. 2 BC**

We have now determined the two possible dates for the birth of Jesus:

1 Aviv (5 April) or 20 Elul (19 September) 2 BC.

The visit of the shepherds

Luke 2:8-16 And there were in the same country (near Bethlehem) shepherds abiding in the field, keeping watch over their flock by night. And, lo, an angel of Yahweh came upon them, and the glory of Yahweh shone round about them: and they were sore afraid. And the angel said unto them, Fear not: for, behold, I bring you good tidings of great joy, which shall be to all people. For unto you is born this day in the city of David a Saviour, which is the Messiah, the Lord. And this shall be a sign unto you; you shall find the babe wrapped in swaddling clothes, lying in a manger. And suddenly there was with the angel a multitude of the heavenly host praising God, and saying: Glory to God in the highest, and on earth peace, good will toward men!

And it came to pass, as the angels were gone away from them into heaven, the shepherds said one to another, Let us now go even unto Bethlehem, and see this thing which is come to pass, which Yahweh has made known unto us. And they came with haste, and found Miryam, and Joseph, and the babe lying in a manger.

We know that the shepherds were in the field with their flock when Jesus was born.

In the Mishnah (Tractate Beitza, c.5) we read that domestic animals were taken away about the time of Passover (Pesach), they fed in the pastures in the summer, and were returned in the fall at the first rain. The first rains usually come just after Sukkot, the last festival in the fall. That is towards the end of September.[124]

They put Jesus in a crib. If it was winter there would be more than enough space in the inns (people didn't travel in the winter) – but the animals would be inside and there would be food in the manger. In spring – especially near a festival like Pesach – the inns would be full and the animals in the field.

Conclusion:

Both calculated dates (5 April and 19 September) are possible for the visit of the shepherds. But the later date is very unlikely, because the rainy season had started and they most probably would not be in the field.

The registration / census of Quirinius

Luk 2:1-5 And it came to pass in those days, that there went out a decree from Caesar Augustus, that the whole Roman Empire should be registered. v2 (This registration was first made when Quirinius was governor of Syria.) v3. And all went to be registered, every one into his own city. v4 And Joseph also went up from Galilee, out of the city of Nazareth, into Judea, unto the city of David, which is called Bethlehem; because he was of the house and lineage of David, to be registered with Miryam his espoused wife, who was pregnant.

Luk 2:6-7 And so it was, that, while they were there, the days were accomplished that she should be delivered. v7 And she brought forth her firstborn son, and wrapped him in swaddling clothes, and laid him in a manger; because there was no room for them in the inn.

---

[124] People always prayed for rain during Sukkot. There is even a Messianic prophecy that says that the nation that does not go up to Jerusalem for Sukkot will not get rain, (Zec 14:17).

The only logical reason why Joseph would travel to Bethlehem with his wife in an advanced stage of pregnancy, is because they had to because of the registration.

The registration that Luke refers to was in 2 BC. Archaeologist and chronologist Gerard Gertoux gives convincing evidence that Quirinius was the governor of Syria from 3 to 2 BC.[125] (Other archaeologists/chronologists like Bergmann, Mommsen and Zumpt confirm it). The historian Paul Orosius dates the registration of August in the year 752 of Rome, which was in 2 BC.[126]

Caesar Augustus was declared "Father of the Land" (Pater Patriae) on 5 February 2 BC. He decreed a registration of the whole Roman Empire (which they considered to be the whole world). It was called the "breviarium totius imperii" ("Inventory of the World"). Basically it was a balance sheet showing all the resources in the entire Roman Empire. The first version of this Breviarium was displayed in the temple of Mars Ultor on 12 May 2 BC.

The registration was probably in March and April. In February it was still too cold and wet (that is why the Romans went to war not earlier than March). And it had to be finished some time before 12 May to give them sufficient time to do the inventory.

If Jesus was born on 20 Elul (19 September), then it means that Joseph intentionally waited until his wife was towards the end of her pregnancy before they travelled to go and register, which doesn't make sense. It also would have been after the registration.

Conclusion:
Jesus was born on 1 Aviv (5 April) 2 BC.

Note: The reason why the Hebrew dates are shown, is because of their significance. The theme and significance of the Biblical date of 1 Aviv for the date of birth of Jesus is amazing (see Part 4).

---

[125] Gérard Gertoux, *Herod the Great and Jesus - Chronological, Historical and Archaeological Evidence*, (Lulu.com, 2017), 21 - 24

[126] Histories against the pagans VI:22:1; VII:3:4

The visit of the wise men[127]

The Sign in heaven

Gen 49:9 Judah is a young lion: from the prey, my son, thou art gone up. He stretches himself and lays down, like a lion and as a lioness. Who shall dare to disturb him?

Why did the wise men interpret the conjunctions as the birth of the "King of the Jews"? Being learned men from Persia (Babylon) they should have been familiar with the prophecies of Balaam and Daniel.

Balaam was a famous pagan prophet. He saw Israel as a lion. He prophesied about a coming Ruler of Israel, which he called a Star:

Num 24:9 He stretches himself and lays down, like a lion and as a lioness. Who shall dare to disturb him? Blessed is he who blesses thee, and cursed is he who curses thee!

Num 24:17a I shall see him, but not now: I shall behold him, but not nigh: there shall come a Star out of Jacob, and a Sceptre shall rise out of Israel.

Leo (with the bright king-star Regulus) is the "King" constellation. It was associated with Judah[128] (Lion of Judah) and royalty.

Daniel was a great and famous prophet. Nebuchadnezzar, the king of Babylon, made him ruler over the whole province of Babylon.[129] It was the metropolis of the Babylonian Empire.

---

[127] In Greek they were called "Magos" (The origin of the English word "magician"). They were learned astronomers who practiced astrology and sorcery (like the Chaldeans). In some translations they are called "Magi".

[128] The symbol of the Roman Empire was the eagle.

[129] His tomb was in Mosul in Iraq (the modern day name for Babylon).
It was a much-visited holy place for Islamic, Christian and Jewish pilgrims - until it was blown up by ISIS (an Islamic terrorist group) in 2014. They also destroyed the shrine of the prophet Jonah.

He also made him chief of the governors over all the wise men of Babylon. He did this because Daniel could interpret his dreams, and none of the astrologers in his empire could do it (Dan 2:48).

Daniel prophesied about an Anointed one that was coming. He gave some calculations when this Anointed one would come (Dan 9), and it was about time. Both kings and prophets were anointed for their roles. Thus they were expecting the birth of the "King of the Jews". (Another reason why they didn't go to Rome, the capital of the Roman Empire).

The lion was the emblem on the tribal sign of Judah. When the Israelites camped in the wilderness they camped on the eastern side of the Tabernacle – under their banner with the lion on it:

> Num 2:2-3 Every man of the children of Israel shall pitch by his own standard, with the ensign of their father's house: far off about the tabernacle of the congregation shall they pitch. And on the east side toward the rising of the sun shall they of the standard of the camp of Judah pitch throughout their armies: and Nachshon the son of Amminadab shall be captain of the children of Judah.

When the wise men saw the "Star of the King of the Jews" (the brightest "star" that they had ever seen!) and realized that Daniel's prophecy came to fulfilment, they naturally would have wanted to go and bless this Lion so that they also would be blessed!

The conjunctions of 3 and 2 BC:

The only astronomical phenomena that satisfactorily fit the description of what the wise men saw, and which would make them call it the "Star of the King of the Jews, were the conjunctions of Venus and Jupiter and the "crowning" of the "King Star" by Jupiter in 3 and 2 BC.[130]

---

[130] See *Venus and Jupiter conjunction: The "Star of Bethlehem"* on page 52 for a description of how spectacular it was.

12 August / 1 Elul 3 BC: "Star in the East"

Conjunction of Jupiter and Venus right in front of the Leo constellation, near the star Regulus (the "King Star"). It was visible on the eastern horizon just before sunrise.

This was on the 50th day after the conception of Miryam.

14 September 3 BC, 17 February 2 BC and 8 May 2 BC: "The Crowning of the King Star"

14 September 3 BC: Jupiter came into conjunction with Regulus (the King Star in the Leo constellation) and then moved passed it. Then it appeared to stop and move backwards until it passed Regulus a second time on 17 February 2 BC. It kept moving until the 23rd March 2 BC where it stopped near Regulus.

From 23 March to 5 April Jupiter stood still for 14 days (14 is the number for David, the king of Israel).

Jupiter then moved again and passed Regulus for a third time on 8 May 2 BC, almost as if it was "crowning" Regulus.[131]

17 June 2 BC: "Star of Bethlehem"

Venus and Jupiter

*Mat 2:1-2 Now after Yeshua was born in Bethlehem of Judea in the days of Herod the king, behold, there came wise men from the East to Jerusalem, and asked: Where is he who is born King of the Jews? For **we have seen his star in the East**, and have come to worship him.*

---

[131] It is called "retrograde motion"

*Mat 2:8-10 And he (Herod) sent them to Bethlehem, and said: Go and search diligently for the young child; and when you have found him, bring me word again, that I may come and worship him also. v9 When they had heard the king, they departed; and, lo, **the star, which they saw in the east,** went before them, till it came and stood over where the young child was. v10 When they saw the star, they rejoiced with exceeding great joy.*

Due to the earth's rotation, stars appear to rise in the east, move across south[132] to set in the west. The first time the wise men saw the conjunction it was on 12 August 3 BC in the east. In the afternoon and evening of 17 June it was in the west.

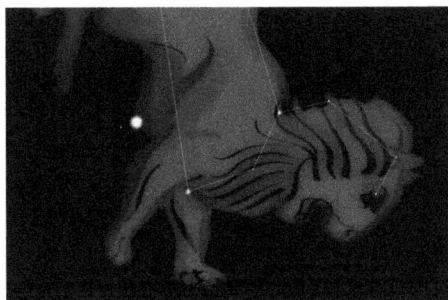

The conjunction of Venus and Jupiter on 16 June 2 BC was an extremely close conjunction (from certain viewpoints they occulted/overlapped).

They appeared to have been one bright shining light.

Bethlehem is about 6 miles from Jerusalem. It would take the wise men not more than about 2 hours on camel (or by foot) to get there. Jerusalem is to the north of Bethlehem. If they saw the conjunction in the west, then it means that they turned to their right when they entered Bethlehem, in order to get to the house where Jesus and his parents lived.[133]

They did not have to wait till evening to see the conjunction: Venus and Jupiter can often be seen in daylight.[134]

---

[132] Except when observed from the equator. This phenomena can be clearly seen with astronomical software (e.g. Stellarium) when time is accelerated. (For old computers try Version 0.12.9.)

[133] They went to live in Bethlehem AFTER the presentation at the Temple.

[134] The only other planet that is also sometimes visible in daytime is Mars, although it's difficult to see:
[https://earthsky.org/astronomy-essentials/10-surprising-things-to-see-in-the-daytime-sky]

On 17 June the conjunction of these 2 bright planets was clearly visible from at least an hour before sunset.

They rejoiced with "exceeding great joy" when they saw the "star" again (Mat 2:10). They saw the "star" in the east the previous year, then they didn't see it, and then they saw it again – which is exactly how the 2 conjunctions on 12 August 3 BC and 17 June 2 BC would have appeared to an ancient observer!

Both conjunctions of Jupiter and Venus took place near and just above Regulus. That is why the wise men thought that it was the same star. Regulus is the "king star" in the constellation of Leo. That is why they called it the "star of the King of the Jews".

If they had any doubts after they saw the first conjunction, then the "Crowning of the King Star" surely would have convinced them!

Comparing the calculated dates for the visit of the wise men

Mat 2:11 And when they (the wise men) came into the house, they saw the young Child with Miryam his mother, and fell down, and worshipped him: and when they had opened their treasures, they presented unto him gifts; gold, and frankincense, and myrrh.

Mat 2:12-14 And being warned of God in a dream that they should not return to Herod, they departed into their own country another way. v13 And when they were departed, behold, an angel of Yahweh appears to Joseph in a dream, saying: Arise, and take the young child and his mother, and flee into Egypt, and be thou there until I bring thee word: for Herod will seek the young child to destroy him. v14 When he arose, he took the young child and his mother by night, and departed into Egypt.

Mat 2:15 And they were there until the death of Herod: that it might be fulfilled which was spoken of Yahweh by the prophet, saying: Out of Egypt have I called my son.

God warned the wise men not to return to Herod. It had to be during the night of the evening that they visited Jesus, otherwise they would be back at him the next day.

The wise men departed the next day. That night Joseph and Miryam fled to Egypt. They stayed there until the death of Herod.[135]

That means that the wise men could not had visited Jesus before his parents took him to the Temple to present him as the firstborn to Yahweh. If they did, then he could not have been back in Israel in time for his presentation.

The presentation at the Temple took place at the earliest 41 days after birth, and then they still had to go back home. That means that Jesus would have been at least 42 days old if the wise men visited them on the very day that they returned back home.

> Lev 12:3-4 And in the eighth day the flesh of his foreskin shall be circumcised. And she shall then continue in the blood of her purifying three and thirty days; she shall touch no set apart thing, nor come into the sanctuary, until the days of her purifying be fulfilled.

> Luk 2:22 And when the days of her purification according to the Instructions of Moshe were accomplished, they brought him to Jerusalem, to present him to Yahweh;

The 2 calculated dates for the birth of Jesus, based on the priestly courses, are 5 April and 19 September in 2 BC. 42 days after 5 April is 17 May, and 42 days after 19 September is 31 October.

If date of birth 5 April:
The wise men visit on or after 17 May

During May Herod was in Jerusalem in his summer palace. His son Antipater was on trial for a conspiracy against him. He sailed to Israel for the trial.[136] Ships didn't sail during winter.[137]

---

[135] They fled in June 2 BC, Herod died on 28 January 1 BC. It was in the same Biblical year.

[136] Jewish Antiquities 17.5

[137] The captain of the ship that Saul was on took a chance to sail in winter. They got shipwrecked (Acts 27).

People would not travel far in winter because of the rain and the snow. Jesus even told his disciples to pray that they would not have to flee in winter (Mat 24:20).

Herod and Quintilius Varus sat together in Jerusalem for the court case. Varus was the new governor of Syria and was on his way to Antioch. Governors were appointed on 1st January. They had to leave Rome before 1 June to go to where they were assigned.[138]

The period after 17 May is confirmed by the "Star of Bethlehem" on 17 June.

The wise men probably left Babylon after they saw Jupiter passing Regulus the third time[139] (8 May 2 BC). By that time they must have realized that the birth of this King of the Jews must be something extraordinary.

They must have reached Jerusalem at the latest on the morning of 17 June 2 BC.[140] When they reached Bethlehem in the afternoon or evening of 17 June 2 BC they saw that famous conjunction, the Star of Bethlehem.

The wise men told Herod that they had seen the star of the King of the Jews in the east. It was the conjunction of Jupiter and Venus that took place on 12 August the previous year[141]

Herod was probably in a very bad mood because his son Antipater conspired against him to take over his throne (Herod eventually had him killed). He was not going to allow anybody else to even try it. He did not want to take any changes. He decided to kill all the little boys up to 2 years of age in the Bethlehem area. He tried his best to ensure that the new King would be eliminated.

---

[138] Josephus, Jewish Antiquities XVII:254-255,
    Cassius Dio: Roman History LVII:14:5; LX:11:6; LX:17:3).
[139] See *The Crowning of the King Star* on page 74
[140] Probably a day or two before: They were searching for Jesus in Jerusalem when Herod heard about it and spoke to them.
[141] That conjunction was proclaiming the conception that had taken place 50 days earlier.

The 2 year limit was a very safe and practical choice for Herod: It definitely would include all children born in the time period that the wise men talked about. Boys of two years old are also easily recognisable – they are no longer in diapers, can talk sentences and are running around – a lot!

If date of birth 19 September:
The wise men visit on or after 31 October

31 October or later is almost an impossible time for the wise men's visit. First of all it was almost winter (It would take them at least two weeks to get back to their home country).

Furthermore, Herod would be in his winter palace in October. His winter palace[142] was in Jericho, which was his capital.

It was the rainy season. He was very sick during the last few months of his life. He probably suffered for months, if not years. Medical doctors have diagnosed him with such horrible diseases that I don't even want to describe here.[143]

There is no significant astronomical event that could be considered to be the *Star of Bethlehem* between 31 October 2 BC and 28 January 1 BC. There was no bright conjunction of the same planets in the same constellation that was seen the previous year in the east.

> ### Conclusion:
> Jesus was born on 1 Aviv/Nissan (5 April) of 2 BC,
> and the wise men visited him on 17 June.

These dates are in harmony with all the facts and they are not contradicted by any historical events.

---

[142] He named it "Cypros Palace" in memory of his mother

[143] Amanda Onion (2017). Researchers Diagnose Herod the Great. *abcNEWS, 25 January 2017.*

Part 4: Chronology and significance of dates

They say that "coincidence" is God's way of remaining anonymous. When there are a series of particular events that happen at specific times, then we can clearly see the Hand of God.

It is amazing how the message of the stars confirms the Biblical chronology. We can almost determine the date of birth of Jesus just by looking at the astronomical events alone! The dates of the astronomical events tell us a wonderful story - but ONLY if we use the calculated dates for his conception and birth according to this book! (For this reason I consider it as divine confirmation that the calculated dates are correct).

In this chronology the historical and astronomical events are listed from the end of the priestly course of Abijah (when the birth of John, the forerunner of the Messiah, was announced), up to the heliacal rising of the star Tsemech (which points to the return of the Messiah).

These are my interpretations. They are based on Biblical symbolism, the meanings of numbers and the numerical values of words

25 January 3 BC:
Prepare the Way

Zachariah went home at the end of his week of duties at the Temple. His wife Elizabeth became pregnant with John (Yochanan).

He will prepare the way for the Messiah:

> Mat 11:10 For this is he, of whom it is written: Behold, I send my messenger before thy face, which shall prepare thy way before thee.

23 June 3 BC:
Conception of Miryam

Gabriel, the messenger of God, visits Miryam and tells her that she will give birth to the Messiah. She became pregnant.

2 July 3 BC:

The Messenger of God announces in the stars that the Word (Torah) became flesh.

Joh 1:14a And the Word was made flesh, and dwelt among us

Mercury conjunction with Regulus in Leo

Explanation of interpretation:

Miryam became pregnant on the day when Gabriel told her that she will be the mother of the Messiah.[144] Gabriel is an angel and messenger of God. Mercury is called the "messenger of the gods". God in Hebrew is Elohim. It is also the Hebrew word for "gods".

This was the 10th day after the conception of Miryam. The number 10 points to the Word of God, because the *Ten Words* is the *Covenant Agreement* of God with us:

> *Exo 34:28b And He wrote upon the tables the words of the Covenant, the Ten Words[145].*

28 July 3 BC:

The Messiah is King, the Son of God.

Sun in conjunction with Regulus in Leo.

This is 26 days after the announcement in the stars that the Word became flesh.

Explanation of interpretation:

The Sun represents the Supreme Being, the God of the Universe.

26 is the numerical value for Yahweh, the Name of God.

---

[144] According to the chronology of this book
[145] "Devarim" means "words". (Unfortunately it is often translated as "commandments".)

12 August / 1 Elul 3 BC:
The Star of the King of the Jews in the east.

The Righteous Bright Morning Star,
the High Priest from the Order of Melchizedek,
is coming to bring deliverance to the captives.

50 days after the conception of Miryam the wise men saw the Star of the King of the Jews rising in the east.[146] It was the conjunction of Venus and Jupiter near Regulus in the constellation Leo.

Explanation of interpretation:

Venus is the bright morning star. Jesus is called the Bright Morning Star (Rev 22:16). Jupiter is Tzedek ("Righteous") in Hebrew. Regulus is the King Star. King is melech in Hebrew, and King of Righteousness is Melchizedek in Hebrew. Jesus is the High Priest after the order of Melchizedek (Heb 5:8-10, 6:20).

50 is associated with the Jubilee, when slaves are set free and debts are cancelled. When Jesus started his ministry he read from Isa 61:1 about the captives being set free, and he said that he fulfilled that prophecy (Luk 4:19).

50 is also referring to the Feast of Weeks (Heb: "Shavuot"). In Judaism it is believed that God gave the Ten Words on this day. This feast is also called "Pentecost", which means 50th. Jesus told his disciples to go to Jerusalem and wait until they were equipped with Power from above. This happened on Pentecost with they were filled with the Holy Spirit (Luk 24:49, Act 1:8, 2:1-4). This was 50 days after Pesach or Passover

This happened on the first day of the Hebrew month of Elul. Elul is an acronym for "I am my beloved's and my beloved is mine". It is a quote from Song of Songs 6:3. These words are often inscribed on wedding rings. Every day during the month of Elul the shofar is blown until the first day of Tishri when it is the Feast of Trumpets.

---

[146] In Judaism it is believed that "when the Messiah shall be revealed, a bright and shining star shall arise in the east" (Zohar in Exod. fol.3.3, 4. & in Numb fol. 85.4 & 86.1). See also Gill's commentary on Num 24:17.

1 October / 22 Tishrei 3 BC:
It's a new beginning.
Jesus the Fountain of Living Water is coming for those who are thirsty.

In 3 BC the heliacal rising[147] of Tsemech, the *Star of the Messiah*, was on 22 Tishrei of the Biblical calendar. 22 Tishrei is the 8th day, the last day of Sukkot (Feast of Tabernacles). This day is called "Shemini Atzeret" in Hebrew. It means the "eighth day of assembly".

Lev 23:36 Seven days you shall offer an offering made by fire unto Yahweh. On the eighth day shall be an holy convocation unto you; and you shall offer an offering made by fire unto Yahweh. It is a solemn assembly; and you shall do no servile work therein.

Explanation of interpretation:

The numerical value of Ἰμσοΰς, the name of Jesus in Greek, is 888. The number 8 symbolizes a new beginning.

2 Cor 5:17 Therefore if any man be in the Messiah, he is a new creature: old things are passed away; behold, all things are become new.

A particular feature of Shemini Atzeret is the *Prayer for rain* (Geshem). It was on that day that Jesus cried out that those who are thirsty must come to him:

Psa 63:1 A Psalm of David, when he was in the wilderness of Judah. O God, Thou art my God; early will I seek Thee: my soul thirsts for Thee, my flesh longs for Thee in a dry and thirsty land, where no water is.

Joh 7:37-38 In the last day, that great day of the feast, Yeshua stood and cried, saying: If any man thirst, let him come unto me, and drink. He who believes in me, as the scripture has said: out of his belly shall flow rivers of living water.

---

[147] See *Astronomical time units* on page 20 for explanation of heliacal rising.

21 March 2 BC:

A very important event regarding the Messiah of Israel was about to happen...

Just after sunset on the evening of 20 March 2 BC the star Tsemech rose together with the full moon.

Explanation of interpretation:

The vernal equinox was on 21 March in 2 BC. Jewish days begin in the evening after sunset, so 21 March (Biblically speaking) begins on the evening of 20 March after sunset.

The Biblical year starts on the first new moon after the vernal equinox.

The first day of the year is on the first day of the month called Aviv (Nissan).

The star Tsemech is the sheaf of ripened barley in the hand of the virgin. Ripened barley is called "aviv" in Hebrew.

Tsemech represents the Messiah, spring, the coming barley harvest and the coming new year.[148]

Seeing the full moon and Tsemech together at the Vernal Equinox is very significant. The full moon represents Israel.[149]

It was a sign that the coming New Year was going to be very important to Israel, and that it had something to do with their Messiah...

---

[148] More fully explained in the chapters "The Star of the Messiah: The Branch in the hand of the Virgin" (page 55) and "Tsemech, the spring star of the barley harvest" (page 57).

[149] In Judaism the moon represents Israel, and the sun the nations of the world. The total solar eclipse over America on 21 August 2017 (dubbed "The Great American Eclipse" by the media), was seen as a message to the world.

14 September 3 BC, 17 February 2 BC and 8 May 2 BC:
The Crowning of the Son of David:
Melchizedek, the King of Righteousness

Heb 1:8 but unto the Son He says: Thy throne, O God, is for ever and ever, the scepter of your kingdom is a scepter of justice.

14 September 3 BC: Jupiter came into conjunction with Regulus and then moved passed it. Then it appeared to stop and move backwards until it passed Regulus a second time on 17 February 2 BC. It kept moving until the 23th March 2 BC where it stopped near Regulus.

From 23 March to 5 April Jupiter stood still for 14 days near Regulus.

Jupiter then moved again and passed Regulus for a third time on 8 May 2 BC.

Explanation of interpretation:

Regulus is the "King Star" in the Leo constellation. The Hebrew name for Jupiter is "Tzedeck". Tzedek means "righteousness". "King of" is "Melchi" in Hebrew. When Jupiter is near Regulus in Leo, then it may be a message about Melchizedek. In this event it is, because it stood still for 14 days.

14 is the number for David, the king of Israel.

The backwards and return movements of Jupiter is called "retrograde motion". It almost appears as if Jupiter is "crowning" Regulus, the "King Star".

It is significant that the wise men enquired about "he who is born King of the Jews". They did not asked to see a prince or the son of a king:

Mat 2:2 (the wise men) asked: Where is he who is born King of the Jews? For we have seen his star in the East, and have come to worship him.

In other words, **Jesus was a King from his birth!**

1 Aviv (Nissan) / 5 April 2 BC:
Birth of Jesus the Messiah

1 Aviv is a very significant date. On this date:
- The Tabernacle was erected[150],
- The priestly service started,
- Regnal years for Jewish kings were calculated.

17 June 2 BC:

Star of Bethlehem:
Confirming the day that Abraham saw

The wise men visited Jesus. They saw the "same star" again.

Explanation of interpretation:

Jupiter (Tzedek) stood still for 14 days, from 23 March to 5 April, the date of birth of Jesus Christ. Then it moves again so that it conjuncts with Venus, the morning star, on the 75th day after Jesus's birth.

This was the conjunction that the wise men saw in Bethlehem when they visited Jesus. They thought that it was "the same star" that they saw in the east the previous year. That is because both conjunctions between Jupiter and Venus were very close and near the star Regulus in the constellation Leo.

The number 75 is very significant:

Abraham was 75 years old when God told him that He will make him a great nation (Gen 12).

Jesus said that Abraham rejoiced when he saw his day (John 8:56).

75 is the numerical value for "heylel" (הילל), the bright morning star.

---

[150] Exodus 40

31 August / 1 Elul 2 BC:

The second witness to confirm the date of birth of Jesus.

And that he will leave for a period of time...

Rev 22:16 I Yeshua have sent mine angel to testify unto you these things in the assemblies. I am the root and the offspring (Tsemech) of David, and the bright and morning star (Jupiter and Venus conjunction near regulus in Leo).

75 days later it was the heliacal setting of Tsemech on 31 August, with the new moon next to it. Tsemech was the second witness[151] to confirm the date of birth of Jesus.

Explanation of interpretation:

We have already mentioned that the Hebrew word "heylel" means bright or shining and that it is used to refer to Venus. But it can also refer to describe the star Tsemech, because Tsemech is also called a "bright star".

The fact that its heliacal setting was 75 days after the Star of Bethlehem, which was on the 75th day after the birth of Jesus, support this association.

The departure of the Bridegroom:

31 August 2 BC was on the first day of Elul. We have looked on the association of the month of Elul with the Bridegroom (page 82).

The heliacal setting of Tsemech was together with a new moon. He was not going to be visible for some time. Jesus said that he is the Bridegroom that was going away:

Mar 2:20 But the days will come, when the Bridegroom shall be taken away from them, and then shall they fast in those days.

---

[151] See *The two bright stars that proclaimed the birth of Jesus* on page 54

1 October / 2 Tishrei 2 BC:

The Bridegroom will return with the sound of the trump

Hos 6:2 After two days will he revive us: in the third day he will raise us up, and we shall live in his sight.

The heliacal rising (return) of Tsemech was on 2 Tishrei in 2 BC.

Explanation for interpretation:

2 Tishrei is the second day of Yom Teruah, the Feast of Trumpets.

Yom Teruah is also called *The Feast of which no man knows the day or the hour*. This is because in ancient times an extra day was sometimes added when the crescent moon was not sighted on the calculated day.[152]

Other appointed times or feasts were later in the month. They could be determined as soon as the new moon was proclaimed. But this was not possible for the Feast of Trumpets, because it started on the first day of the month.

It is believed that Jesus is coming back on the Feast of Trumpets, because he said that *nobody knows the day or the hour* when he is coming back. It is a Jewish idiom for Yom Teruah. It is also the next appointed time that Jesus has to fulfill.

Mat 25:13 Watch therefore, for you know neither the day nor the hour wherein the Son of man comes.

---

[152] Dates in his book are based on the probability of the crescent moon being visible. That is usually about 15 to 20 hours after the calculated astronomical new moon. This was also the system in place during the Second Temple period:

The Sanhedrin would calculate the date when the crescent moon should be visible. The witnesses would only confirm the date on the calculated date.

If the crescent room was sighted, or if it was on the 30th of a month, then the new month would be declared, starting from that evening.

If a witness testified that he saw the moon before the calculated time, he was considered to be a false witness.

Part 5: Ages and dispensations

Precession of the equinoxes: The Great Year and Ages

Ecc 3:11 He has made everything beautiful in his time: also he has set the age (or world) in their heart, so that no man can find out the work that God makes from the beginning to the end.

Astrological ages (referred to by theologians as "dispensations") are determined by the vernal equinox. Because the solar and sidereal years are not exactly the same length, the constellations behind the rising sun on the date of the vernal equinox slowly moves backwards to the previous (preceding) constellation. This is called precession of the vernal equinox.[153]

Ages are named after the constellations in which the sun appears at the vernal equinox. An astrological age is about 2000 years (an average of 2150 years if you use the 12 ancient zodiac signs, or an average of 1985 years if you use all 13 constellations).

One complete cycle of the equinoxes around the ecliptic takes about 25,800 years and is called the Great Year. It is also called the Platonic Year in honour of Plato (he used the term "perfect year" to describe the return of the celestial bodies to their original positions).

Symbolism

Symbolism is very much an universal language, which is why astrologers and dream interpreters often come to the same conclusions as theologians.

When we compare the symbolism of stars, constellations and their signs with the corresponding symbols in the Bible, within the historical time frames of astronomical ages, then an amazing prophetic message unfold in the heavens.

---

[153] This is not to be confused with the wobbling of the earth's axis, which is also called "precession".

On the first day of each of the 4 seasons one of the 12 constellations will be behind the sun. The 4 constellations are related to the one that indicates the current age. They tell an amazing story:

The 4 cardinal signs or constellations are the equinoxes and solstices.[154] The word *cardinal* comes from the Latin word for *hinge*, because they marked the change in seasons. The *vernal equinox* determine the age. What is truly amazing is how the 4 cardinal points synchronize with each other during an age. They are like a big astronomical clock in the sky.

Ages change after about 2000 years due to the backwards movement (precession) of the constellations, as seen at the vernal equinox. But the change in constellation alone doesn't give us exact dates. Astrologers and theologians usually use certain events that define and represent the age. Changing of ages are usually accompanied by very rare astronomical events, like specific occultations (when Jesus was born) or five star stelliums (a close alignment of planets within a constellation, at the time when Abraham was born and at the dawn of Aquarius/New Age).

There is not consensus between astrologers about the exact dates when an age starts or finishes, because people use different borders for the constellations to determine the ages. Usually events that happen during the transitions between ages are used to give more accurate dates (e.g. the destruction of the Second Temple, the birth of Jesus or an unusual astronomical event).

We are at the end of the Church age (Pisces) and are entering the "New Age" called Aquarius. That means that the return of Jesus is at hand. Yes there is a "New Age" coming - but it is not the one that the world is expecting! It will only seem as if things are going their way in the beginning. All this has been prophesied in the Bible thousands of years ago.

---

[154] Or: the 4 cardinal points of the ecliptic are the 2 equinoctial and the 2 solstitial points.

The Greek word for age is "aiōn" and it refers to very long time periods. In Hebrew it is "olam". In many translations it is sometimes translated as "world" as in "world to come" (Our physical world is called "eretz" in Hebrew and "kosmos" in Greek). The Jews call the Messianic Age (when Jesus will rule as Messiah) "Olam Haba". It is also translated as "ever" or "always and forever".

Theologians often refer to three progressive dispensations or stages in God's redemption of mankind: Patriarchal, Mosaic and Church (or Christian). The Mosaic dispensation follows the Patriarchal dispensation. The two together run concurrent with the Age of Aries. During the Age of Aries the sacrificial system was in place and the patriarchs and Israelites sacrificed rams and goats.

The Church Age runs concurrent with the Age of Pisces. Paul calls the Church Age the "dispensation of the fullness of times" when he refers to the time period before the end of that age:

> Eph 1:9-10 Having made known unto us the mystery of his will, according to his good pleasure which he has purposed in himself: That in the dispensation of **the fullness of times** he might gather together in one all things in the Messiah, both which are in heaven, and which are on earth; even in him.

The Church Age is also called the "Age of the Gentile Nations":

> Luk 21:24 And they shall fall by the edge of the sword, and shall be led away captive into all nations, and Jerusalem shall be trampled down by the Gentiles, until the end of the age of the Gentiles.

> Luk 21:25-26 And there shall be signs in the sun and moon and stars; and on the earth fear among the nations, bewildered at the roaring of the sea and the waves. People's expectation of the things which are going to happen to the world will make them faint because of fear, for the powers of heaven shall be shaken.

> Luk 21:27 And then shall they see the Son of man coming in a cloud with power and great glory.

The Age of Aries: Age of Covenants and Sacrifices

The Man who brings Water
Aquarius

Two fishes — *Pisces*   **(Scape)goat** — *Capricorn*

Ram (Lamb) — *Aries*   **Archer / Hunter** — *Sagittarius*

♈ T — *Bull / Tauris*   **Eagle with snake** — *Scorpio (higher level)*

Earth

Twins — *Gemini*   **Scales of Justice** — *Libra*

Water & Resurrection — *Cancer*   **Virgin** — *Virgo*

Lion

VE: Vernal Equinox, FE: Fall Equinox, SS: Summer Solstice, WS: Winter Solstice

Aries: 1953 BC - Stellium - Abraham

Abbreviations: VE: Vernal Equinox, FE: Fall Equinox, SS: Summer Solstice, WS: Winter Solstice

Age Constellation sign Aries: The Ram, Lamb of God

The Patriarchal and Mosaic dispensations correspond with Aries, the Age of the Ram. It started when Abraham sacrificed a ram, and it ended with the Lamb of God (Jesus) being crucified.

Gen 15:6 And he (Abraham) believed in Yahweh; and He counted it to him for righteousness.

*Gen 15:9 And He said unto him: Take me an heifer of three years old, and a she goat of three years old, and a **ram** of three years old, and a turtledove, and a young pigeon.*

Gen 15:10 And he took unto him all these, and divided them in the midst, and laid each piece one against another: but the birds divided he not.

Gen 15:17 And it came to pass, that, when the sun went down, and it was dark, behold a smoking furnace, and a burning lamp that passed between those pieces.

Gen 15:18 **In the same day Yahweh made a covenant with Abram**, *saying: Unto thy seed have I given this land, from the river of Egypt unto the great river, the river Euphrates*

Jesus is sometimes depicted as a lamb (ram) with a cross. It symbolizes the end of the Age of Aries and the beginning of the Age of Pisces.

The Age of Aries is also the **Age of Covenants**. A ram was usually cut in half when a covenant was made.

Gen 22:7-8 And Isaac spoke unto Abraham his father, and said: My father: and he said: Here am I, my son. And he said: Behold the fire and the wood: but where is the lamb for a burnt offering? And Abraham said: My son, God (Elohim) will provide himself a lamb for a burnt offering: so they went both of them together.

Joh 1:29 The next day Yochanan saw Yeshua coming unto him and says: Behold the Lamb of God, which takes away the sin of the world!

1 Cor 5:7b For our Pesach lamb has been sacrificed for us, the Messiah.

Paul calls the Covenants of God the **Covenants of the Promise**:

Eph 2:12 That at that time you were without the Messiah, being aliens from the commonwealth of Israel, and strangers from the **Covenants of Promise**, *having no hope, and without God in the world.*

The first covenant was made with Abraham. That covenant was expanded and renewed until the last one that Jesus made at his Passover meal with the disciples.

Capricornus: The Scapegoat

The Scapegoat was sacrificed on Yom Kippur (Day of Atonement). After the death of Jesus the scarlet thread that was tied to the door of the Temple never turned white again, until the Temple was destroyed in 70 AD. (It only turned white when God accepted the Yom Kippur sacrifice).

"The rabbis taught: Forty years before the Temple was destroyed, the lot never came into the right hand, the red wool did not become white, the western light did not burn, and the gates of the Temple opened of themselves". Tract Yomah[155] (Day of Atonement).

That is because Jesus was the final Scapegoat for our sins. When Jesus died it was the end of the Age of Aries. In the Messianic Age there will be no Yom Kippur offerings:

> Jer 3:16 And it shall come to pass, when you be multiplied and increased in the land, in those days, says Yahweh, they shall say no more, The ark of the covenant of Yahweh: neither shall it come to mind: neither shall they remember it; neither shall they miss it; and they won't make another one.

There is no mention of an ark or a Yom Kippur service in the Messianic Temple (Ezekiel chapters 40 to 46).

Libra: God's Instructions and the Scales of Justice

> Pro 11:1 A false balance is an abomination to Yahweh: but a just weight is his delight.

God's Instructions ("Torah" in Hebrew) are represented by the Scales of Justice:

Abraham was chosen because he obeyed God's Instructions / Torah (Gen 26:4-5).

---

[155] Michael L. Rodkinson (1918). *New Edition of the Babylonian Talmud - Original Text Edited, Corrected, Formulated, and Translated into English.* (President Hebrew College, Cincinnati, O). Book 3, Chapter IV, p.60 (p.1541 of PDF)

Beltsasar was weighed but was found too light - Dan 5:27.

Jesus came to fulfill (fully preach, confirm) God's Instructions (Torah), and to die in the place of those who were found too light.[156]

Cancer: Resurrection / Re-birth

Cancer has 4 sign symbols: crab, dolphin, seal or sea lion. In ancient mythology this sign marked the resurrection of the earth from the flood. Maybe they chose the crab because it has 8 legs in remembrance of Noah and his family?

The concept of resurrection and the sea is clearly shown by the basin of bronze in front of the Tabernacle (Exo 30:18). Solomon built a very big one that was called the Sea of Bronze. The priests and everybody who went to the Temple took a ritual bath called a "mikveh" (baptism in English). They were "born again" each time they came out of the water ("resurrected"). The Red Sea crossing of the Israelites is also called a baptism (1 Cor 10:2).

Summary:

The Age of Aries was the age of covenants and sacrifices. The main annual sacrifices was the Pesach Lamb at Passover and the Scapegoat at Day of Atonement (Yom Kippur). All the sacrifices was according to the Torah (represented by Libra). The priests would take a *mikveh* (baptismal bath) before they brought any sacrifices. The *mikveh* symbolized rebirth or resurrection.

The sacrifices and appointed times ("Biblical feasts") were shadows of Jesus who was coming (Col 2:17, Heb 8:5). Jesus made the covenant on behalf of Abraham[157] (Gen 15). The descendants of Abraham did not keep the commandments. They were weighed and found too light and had to die. But Jesus was the one who made the Covenant with God on behalf of Abraham. THAT is why Jesus had to die (Heb 9:15).

---

[156] Mat 5:17, Rom 15:19, Heb 9:15
[157] God changed his name from Abram to Abraham.

The Age of Pisces: The Church Age

The Man who brings Water
Aquarius

Two fishes
Pisces

(Scape)goat
Capricorn

Ram (Lamb)
Aries

Archer / Hunter
Sagittarius

♁ T
Bull / Tauris

Eagle with snake
Scorpio (higher level)

Twins
Gemini

Scales of Justice
Libra

Water & Resurrection
Cancer

Virgin
Virgo

Lion

VE: Vernal Equinox, FE: Fall Equinox, SS: Summer Solstice, WS: Winter Solstice
Earth

Pisces: 2 BC - "Melchizedek Occultation" - Jesus Christ

Abbreviations: VE: Vernal Equinox, FE: Fall Equinox, SS: Summer Solstice, WS: Winter Solstice

The origin of the 1 AD date of birth of Jesus.

It seems that the modern calendar developed by Dionysius Exiguus in the 6th century AD, commencing with the birth of Jesus Christ at AD 1 (according to his calculations), was influenced by precession of the equinoxes and astrological ages.[158]

There are five naked-eye planets — Mercury, Venus, Mars, Saturn and Jupiter. They formed a stellium in the year 2000. Apparently Dionysius considered that as the end of the Church age (Pisces).

---

[158] Sepp Rothwangl (2001). "Consideration of the origin of the yearly count in the Julian and Gregorian calendar". This article was a lecture given at the *"Cosmology though time" International Conference*, held at the Astronomical Observatory of the University of Rome (June 17-21, 2001). Online (9/2018): [http://www.calendersign.com/en/to_adjustment_AD.php]

More references listed at [https://en.wikipedia.org/wiki/Astrological_age]

They believed that an age was 2000 years, so he subtracted 2000 and determined the year 1 AD as the birth of Jesus. It was the beginning of the Age of Pisces and they believed that the age started with the birth of Jesus.

Constellation sign Pisces: Judaism and Christianity

Gal 4:4a but when the appointed time came,
God sent forth his Son...

The death and resurrection of Jesus marked the end of the Age of Aries. His birth marked the dawn of Pisces.[159]

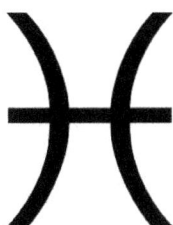

According to astrologers Pisces started in 1 AD.

Many people are familiar with the fish as a Christian symbol. There are 2 fishes in the sign of Pisces, representing both Christianity and Judaism. The two fishes are tied together, but facing away from each other.

They both serve the God of Abraham, but they are not in unity. Jesus said that in him Jew and Gentile are one (Eph 2:12).

Not only did Jesus live during the transition of the ages – he WAS the transition of the ages! This gives new meaning to the song *Rock of Ages*!

Left: Gefilte fish joke plaque.

The plaque refers to a well known Jewish fish dish called "gefilte fish".

It probably was intended as a joke, but it's symbolism fits the sign of Pisces.

Image: WC, Brianhe

---

[159] Note: there is a transition period between ages where they overlap

Image: Fishes representing Pishes (original): Badstudios London, Flickr, Creative Commons (Cropped)

The full price of redemption

The Israelites (males from 20 years and older) had to pay a yearly tribute of half a shekel as ransom money to "make an atonement for your souls" (Exo 30:16, 38:26). It was used for the Temple service.

> Exo 30:16 And thou shall take the atonement money of the children of Israel, and shall appoint it for the service of the tabernacle of the congregation; that it may be a memorial unto the children of Israel before Yahweh, to make an atonement for your souls.

Why did they have to pay half a shekel and not a full shekel? Because only Jesus can give the other half, we need him to make atonement for us. Jesus told Peter to go fishing to get this money for them to pay this tribute:

> Mat 17:27 Notwithstanding, lest we should offend them, go thou to the sea, and cast an hook, and take up the fish that first comes up; and when thou hast opened his mouth, thou shall find a piece of money: that take, and give unto them for me and thee.

Fishers of men

When Jesus called his disciples he said that he will make them fishers of men (Mat 4:19, Mar 1:17). One day some of the disciples went fishing. They caught nothing the whole night. The next morning Jesus was standing on the shore, and he told them to cast the net again:

> Joh 21:6 And he said unto them: Cast the net on the right side of the ship, and you shall find. They cast therefore, and now they were not able to draw it for the multitude of fishes.

> Joh 21:11 Simon Peter went up, and drew the net to land full of great fishes, an hundred and fifty and three: and for all there were so many, yet was not the net broken.

Why was the exact numbers of fish written down? What is the connection between Jesus, fish and the number 153?

Hebrew letters also have numerical values. The numerical numbers of words are called "gematria". The gematria for the Hebrew words for "sons of God" (*Bney HaElohim*) and "I am God" (*Ani Elohim*) is 153.

If you tell somebody about God then you are a "fisher of men", and if he becomes a believer then he is called a "son of God".

So when Jesus caused them to catch 153 fishes, he was confirming his divinity and his command to his disciples to go and preach the gospel.

Gemini (Twins): Esau and Jacob / Rome and the Jews

The twins confirm the symbolism of the two fishes. We read about two sets of twins in the Bible, one of them was Esau and Jacob. Jacob is the other name for Israel (Gen 32:28, 35:10). Esau swore to kill his brother Israel. Esau, the twin brother of Jacob, is also called Edom (Gen 25:30, 36:1). In Rabbinic literature Edom refers to Rome and Christianity.

Esau is one of the ancestors of the Arabs (Gen 28:19, Gen 36). The Jews and Arabs are Semitic nations (descendants of Shem, one of the sons of Noah).

From about 700 BC the Etruscans went to and settled in Italy. They were descendents of Esau.[160] They assimilated into Roman culture and deeply influenced it. The Tarquins, a family of Etruscans, was the last dynastic rulers of Rome.

Herod the Great reinforced the association of Rome with Edom. He was an Edomite raised as a Jew. In 36 BC he conquered Jerusalem and Israel (then called Judea) with the help of the Roman army.

---

[160] Their male gene (Y haplogroup) is prevalent in the Middle East and in the Arab World. By the first century BC Roman citizens probably composed about 20% of them.
www.eupedia.com/forum/threads/25163-Y-DNA-haplogroups-of-ancient-civilizations
www.penn.museum/sites/worlds_intertwined/essay.shtml
Daniel Brinton (1889) "The Ethnologic Affinities of the Ancient Etruscans" (Read before the American Philosophical Society, Oct.18, 1889) 506-527
Online (1/2019): [http://biostor.org/reference/203314]

The other set of twins was Peretz and Zerach, the sons of Judah by Tamar (Gen 38, 1 Chr 2:4). Peretz means "breaching", and Zerach means "rising". After the death of Herod the Great Judea (Israel) was divided (breached) into Judea and Galilea.

It was the rise of the Roman Empire and Christianity. By the 4th century Christianity was Romanized (de-judaized/paganized, syncretized and hellenized), causing a breach between Jews and Christians.

There is a Jewish belief that Messiah will come when you can't differentiate between Jew and Gentile - like identical twins. Since the 1960's (Dawn of Aquarius) many Christians have started to celebrate Biblical feasts and keeping the Sabbath. People often confuse them with Jews because they are following many of the beliefs and practices of Christian[161] believers in the first century.

Edom and the building of the Third Temple

Some Jewish scholars believe that descendants of Edom (Gentiles) will prepare the building of the Third Temple as "compensation" for destroying the Second Temple.

> Zec 6:15a And those who are far off shall come and build in the temple of Yahweh

> Isa 60:10a And the sons of strangers shall build up thy walls, and their kings shall minister unto thee.

Herod the Great, a *descendent of Edom*, did massive building works on the Temple Mount. He wanted to be remembered forever as the builder of the greatest temple of the Jews. He basically rebuilt the Temple that Zerubbabel build, but on a much bigger scale.

The Temple was destroyed in 70 AD and all that remain is part of its foundation (it is called the Kotel or Wailing Wall).

---

[161] In Hebrew speaking communities followers of Jesus were called Nazarenes or People of the Way. In Greek speaking countries they were called Xhristianos.

"It sounds illogical that the Third Jewish Temple will be built by non-Jews," Rabbi Berger told Breaking Israel News. "But Rabbinic sources state explicitly that this is what they must do to fix the historic wrongs that were committed."

Many people believe that US President Donald Trump has already started this process when he decided to move the US embassy to Jerusalem[162] (that's why the Muslims were in uproar).

This will signify the end of the Age of Pisces (ages overlap), because the Messiah will come soon after the antichrist sat in the Temple as God (2 Thes 2:4).

The numerical number of Donald Trump in Hebrew (424) is the same as the words *Moshiach ben David*.

Rabbi Berger says: "But Donald Trump is not righteous enough or knowledgable in Bible to actually be the Messiah. Trump's connection to the Messiah is that he will play a role in one of the major functions of the Messiah. He will pave the way for building the Third Temple."

Virgo: The Star of the Messiah rising in the East

According to ancient Jewish tradition[163] a star will rise in the east when the Messiah is born. Celestial bodies rise in the east, so what is so special about that?

The orientation of earth's axis of rotation gradually shifts in a cycle of approximately 25800 years (it happens concurrent with the precession or backwards movement of the equinox). This "wobble of the earth" is called "axial precession".

When you are facing east, the position of the stars where they "arise" will change due to this axial precession.

---

[162] [www.breakingisraelnews.com/104682/ancient-jewish-sources-indicate-trump-will-pave-way-for-third-temple-prominent-rabbi/]

[163] Zohar: Genesis fol. 74. 3. and Exodus fol. 3. 3, 4 (cited by John Gill in his commentary on Mat 2:2 in his *Exposition on the entire Bible*)

The "Star of the Messiah" rose exactly in the east and set exactly in the west during the reign of the last Jewish king, up to the destruction of the Second Temple.[164]

The next time that it will happen again will only be in about 23000 years from now.[165]

Born of a virgin[166]

Tsemech represents the sheaf of barley in the hand of the Virgin, the Virgo constellation. It is significant that the constellation Virgo is one of the 4 cardinal points during the Age of Pisces.

> Gen 3:15 and I will put enmity between thee and the woman, and between thy seed and **her seed**. He shall bruise thy head, and thou shall bruise his heel.

This is the first prophecy about a virgin birth, because women don't have seed.[167]

> Luk 1:35 And the angel answered and said unto her, The Holy Spirit shall come upon thee, and the power of the Highest (Elyon) shall overshadow thee: therefore also the holy child which shall be born of thee shall be called the Son of God.

> Mat 1:20 But while he considered these things, behold, an angel of Yahweh appeared unto him in a dream, saying: Joseph, thou son of David, fear not to take unto thee Miryam thy wife: for that which is conceived in her is of the Holy Spirit.

---

[164] Herod conquered Jerusalem in 36 BC, and the Temple was destroyed in 70 AD. The star *Tsemech* rose on the "celestial equatorial plane".

[165] In comparison the star Tsemech did not even touch the celestial equator during the time of Bar Korbah, the leader of the Jewish revolt in 135 AD (Many Jews thought that he was the Messiah).

[166] See Appendix D on page 140: *Born of a virgin: Is it possible?*

[167] Her eggs are fertilized by the seed of a man.

The Virgin Bride of the Messiah

The followers of Jesus are collectively known as his Bride[168]:

Isa 61:10 I will greatly rejoice in Yahweh, my soul shall be joyful in my God; for He has clothed me with the garments of salvation. He has covered me with the robe of righteousness, as a Bridegroom decks Himself with ornaments, and as a Bride adorns herself with her jewels.

Joh 3:27-29 Yochanan answered and said: ... You yourselves are my witnesses, that I said: I am not the Messiah, but I have been sent before him. He who has the Bride is the Bridegroom. But the friend of the Bridegroom, who stands and listens to him, rejoices greatly because of the Bridegroom's voice. Therefore this joy of mine is now complete.

2 Cor 11:2 For I am jealous over you with a godly jealousy: for I have espoused you to one Husband, that I may present you as a chaste virgin to the Messiah.

Rev 21:9 And there came unto me one of the seven angels which had the seven vials full of the seven last plagues, and he spoke with me, saying: Come here, I will show thee the Bride, the Lamb's wife.

Rev 22:17 And the Spirit and the Bride say: "Come!". And anyone who hears say: "Come!". And let him who is thirsty come. And whosoever will, let him take the water of life freely.

Many astro-prophets[169] associate the woman in Revelations with the Bride of the Messiah:

Rev 12:1 And there appeared a great sign in heaven: a woman clothed with the sun, and the moon under her feet, and upon her head a crown of twelve stars.

---

[168] A bride is called a "set-apart" or "holy" one in Hebrew. If you think that you are part of the Bride, but you are lawless, then you are making a big mistake!

[169] People who look at the stars in order to make predictions about the second coming of Jesus. They are especially interested in the constellations Leo and Virgo.

Christologies

One of the characteristics of Christianity are its Christologies. Christology is the theological interpretation of the person and work of Christ.[170]

The dominant Christology today probably is the Athanasian Creed of 361 AD. It teaches the concept of the "Triune God" or "Trinity". Its origins was the Nicene Creed of 325 AD when Trinitarianism became the official Christology.

There was no official Christology in the early church. It seems that the Christology of a "Twinity"[171] was the most prevalent in the first three centuries of Christianity[172]. Jesus said the following of him and his Father:

> *John 10:30 I and my Father are one.*
>
> *John 17:11b Holy Father, keep through thine own name those whom Thou has given me, that they may be one, as we are.*
>
> *John 14:9b he who has seen me has seen the Father*

In many verse in the Bible it is impossible to distinguish between Jesus and God the Father. This unique and perfect unity is beautifully reflected in the star Tsemech:

Tsemech is not a normal star, but two very close stars that spins around each other. This wasn't discovered until its light was analyzed with a spectroscope. They are so close together that the two components cannot be distinguished from each other, not even with a very strong telescope. The shape of the two stars in the system are influenced by their gravitational interaction.[173]

---

[170] "Christ" is the transliteration of the Greek "Xhristianos". "Messiah" is the transliteration of the Hebrew "Mashiach". It means "Anointed".

[171] A Christology that only refers to the Father and the Son.

[172] Please note: This chapter is not a debate on christologies. It focuses on the unity between God the Father and his Son Jesus Christ, simply because it is reflected in the binary nature of the star Tsemech. I'm not making a theological statement here about Christologies.

[173] http://www.constellation-guide.com/spica/

Sagittarius: Archer / Bow and arrow

Mat 4:17 From that time Yeshua began to preach, and to say: Repent! For the Kingdom of Heaven is at hand.

Psa 7:13 If a person will not repent, He sharpens his sword. He has bent his bow, and made it ready (to shoot)

The symbolism of the arrow is to aim at something. The Hebrew word "Torah" means "instruction" ("law" is a mistranslation). The meaning of its root is to aim in order to hit the mark. (The root of the Greek word for sin is to miss the mark.)

Jesus came to fully preach the Torah (the same Greek word "pleroo" is used in both Mat 5:17 and Rom 15:19).

The end-time hunters and the diaspora

Jer 16:14 Therefore, behold, the days come, says Yahweh, that it shall no more be said: Yahweh lives, that brought up the children of Israel out of the land of Egypt;

Jer 16:15 But, Yahweh lives, that brought up the children of Israel from the land of the north, and from all the lands whither he had driven them: and I will bring them again into their land that I gave unto their fathers.

Jer 16:16 Behold, I will send for many fishers, says Yahweh, and they shall fish them; and after will I send for many hunters, and they shall hunt them from every mountain, and from every hill, and out of the holes of the rocks.

Hunters use bow and arrows to hunt. The prophecy in Jeremiah points to the end time. God is going to bring back the children of Israel back to their land. The return of Jews from the diaspora to the Land of Israel is called "aliyah". The return of all the Jews to Israel will mark the end of the Age of Pisces.

People and organizations who are involved in helping Jews return to Israel are called fishers. Those who chase them away from their countries (e.g. Hitler) are called hunters.

Satan the dragon, the soul hunter

Eph 6:16 Above all, taking the shield of faith, with which you shall be able to extinguish all the flaming arrows of the wicked.

Evil thoughts and temptations are called the flaming arrows of the wicked. If we don't stop them they will destroy us.

WARNING!

Tomorrow's news today

I've got some good news, and I've got some bad news:

Since the days of the prophet Daniel (about 2500 years ago) it has been prophesied in the Bible that in the end times Satan will rule the whole world for a certain period. It was prophesied that he will defeat those who worship the Living God, and that the whole world will worship him.

This explains why there has been a revival in the pagan religions and Satanism since the dawn of the Age of Aquarius. It is a sign of the end times. Governments of traditional Christian nations are now busy outlawing Christianity and the Bible.[174]

The good news for those who worship Yahweh is that it will be only for a specific time, and then the Messiah will come:

Dan 7:21 I looked and saw that the same horn[175] made war with the saints. He was defeating them;

Dan 2:22 until the Ancient of days came, and judgment was given to the saints of the Most High; and the time came that the saints possessed the kingdom.

---

[174] They do it by portraying the preaching of the Word of God as "hate speech", even though the core of the Bible message is love and kindness - even to your enemies! This war against the Bible becomes more obvious if we consider the fact that they are not against the Koran (the holy book of the Muslims that preaches death to all non-Muslims).

[175] Horns symbolizes rulership/kingship (see also Rev 17:12).

In Greek mythology Sagittarius is associated with a centaur. When people not used to horses saw invading nomads riding on horses for the first time, they thought that they were creatures with the upper body of a human and the lower body and legs of a horse. They probably were archers on horse (like the Mongol horse archers who invaded and took over most of Asia).

Rev 6:2 And I looked and saw a white horse: and he who sat on him had a bow; and a crown was given unto him, and he went forth conquering, and to conquer[176].

Rev 13:4-8 And they worshipped the dragon (Satan) which gave power unto the beast. And they worshipped the beast, saying: "Who is like unto the beast? Who is able to make war with him? v5 And there was given unto him a mouth speaking great things and blasphemies; and power was given unto him to continue for forty-two months. v6 And he opened his mouth in blasphemy against God, to blaspheme his Name and his Tabernacle, and those living in heaven. v7 And it was given unto him to make war with the saints and to defeat them. And power was given him over all kindreds, and tongues, and nations. v8 And all that dwell upon the earth shall worship him, everyone whose name is not written in the book of life of the Lamb slain from the foundation of the world.

The good news:

When the alotted time of Satan, the Antichrist, the Beast, their armies and the wicked people is over Jesus will come (also on a white horse):

Rev 19:11 And I saw heaven opened, and behold a white horse; and he who sat upon him was called Faithful and True. In righteousness he judges and makes war.

Jesus will defeat Satan and those who worship him, as well as all the armies who fight against Israel (Rev 19:11-20:2).

---

[176] Commentators sometimes confuse this destroyer with Jesus because he rides on a white horse. However, the context is the end times, when Satan is given authority to rule and to defeat the followers of Jesus for a certain period.

The Age of Aquarius: The Messianic Age

The Man who brings Water
Aquarius

Two fishes — *Pisces* · V E · **(Scape)goat** — *Capricorn*

Ram (Lamb) — *Aries* · **Archer / Hunter** — *Sagittarius*

✝ T · *Bull / Tauris* · SS · Earth · WS · **Eagle with snake** — *Scorpio (higher level)*

Twins — *Gemini* · FE · **Scales of Justice** — *Libra*

Water & Resurrection — *Cancer* · **Virgin** — *Virgo*

Lion

Aquarius: 2012 BC - Stellium - Dawning Messianic Age

Abbreviations: VE: Vernal Equinox, FE: Fall Equinox, SS: Summer Solstice, WS: Winter Solstice

Astrologers and pagans call it the "New Age". The Messianic Kingdom has been prophesied in the Bible since the Tabernacle was built in the desert in c.1445 BC. Ezekiel and John also refer to it.

Age Constellation sign: The Man who brings water

Jesus: Son of Man and Fountain of Living Water:

> Joh 7:37-38 In the last day, that great day of the feast, Yeshua stood and cried, saying: If any man thirst, let him come unto me, and drink. He who believes in me, as the scripture has said: out of his belly shall flow rivers of living water.

This was on the 8th day of the Feast of Tabernacles. The number 8 speak of new beginnings - like the coming Messianic New Age.

Clouds bring rain and water, so it is fitting that the Man who is called the Fountain of Living Water comes with the clouds:

Dan 7:13 I saw in the night visions, and, behold, one like the Son of man came with the clouds of heaven, and came to the Ancient of days, and they brought him near before Him.

Dan 7:14 And there was given him dominion, and glory, and a kingdom, that all people, nations, and languages, should serve him: his dominion is an everlasting dominion, which shall not pass away, and his kingdom that which shall not be destroyed.

Rev 14:14 And I looked, and behold a white cloud, and upon the cloud one sat like unto the Son of man, having on his head a golden crown, and in his hand a sharp sickle.

Waters were flowing out from under the doorstep of the Temple which Ezekiel saw in his vision (Eze ch. 47). It was a vision of the Temple that will be standing in Jerusalem during the Messianic Age.

This stream of water became a river that ran into the Dead Sea, where it brought life. On the banks of the river fruit trees will grow (Eze 47:5-12).

Taurus (Bull): The Aleph and the Tav (Alpha and Omega)

The bull represents power. The first and last letters of the Hebrew alphabet are used as symbolic signs to represent the bull. In Hebrew they are the "aleph" (Akkadian word for "bull") and the "tav".[177]

Bibles translators use the equivalent of our Latin alphabet, the alpha and omega. In the last chapter in the Bible (Rev 22) Jesus says that he is the Alpha and the Omega - and that he is coming soon! All power has been given unto him.

When Jesus returns the Jews will look at him and mourn when they realize that they crucified their Messiah at his first coming:

---

[177] The capital T is used to represent Taurus, the Bull.

*Zec 12:10 And I will pour upon the house of David, and upon the inhabitants of Jerusalem, the Spirit of grace and of supplications; and they shall look upon **XA** whom they have pierced. And they shall mourn for him, as one mourns for his only son, and their grief for him will be bitter, as the grief for (the death of) a firstborn.*

Rev 1:7 Behold, he comes with clouds; and every eye shall see him, and they also which pierced him: and all kindreds of the earth shall wail because of him. Even so, Amen.

In the Hebrew text it does not say "me" or "him" (some translations add it in italics), it actually says the aleph-tav, which are the two symbols for the bull. The original letter tav is a cross in the ancient Paleo Hebrew (also called Phoenician). A symbolic reading of the Aleph-Tav could be "the strong one on the cross".

Scorpius the Eagle: Snake eater

The Scorpio constellation has more than one symbol. The eagle represents the "more mature" Scorpio, a "higher expression" of Scorpio power.

When God made the Covenant with Israel, He described Himself as an eagle who carried them on his wings:

Exo 19:3 And Moshe went up unto God, and Yahweh called unto him out of the mountain, saying: Thus shall thou say to the house of Jacob, and tell the children of Israel: You have seen what I did unto the Egyptians, and how I bare you on eagles' wings, and brought you unto myself.

The eagle is often depicted with a snake in his claws. Eagles eat snakes. It could also symbolises the angel who is going to bind Satan at the end of days:

Rev 20:1-2 And I saw a angel come down from heaven, having the key of the bottomless pit and a great chain in his hand. And he laid hold on the dragon, that old serpent, which is the Devil, and Satan, and bound him a thousand years.

Leo: Lion of Judah

Rev 5:5 And one of the elders says unto me, Weep not: behold, the Lion of the tribe of Judah, the Root of David, has prevailed to open the book, and to loose the seven seals thereof.

Jesus is called the Lion of the tribe of Judah. When he comes back he will destroy the enemies of Israel.

The Jupiter-Venus conjunction on 17 June 2 BC in the constellation Leo is called "The Star of Bethlehem".[178] As it was setting in the west, it was preceded by Mars and Mercury.

First there will be wars: Mars is the god of war.

There will be prophets like Elijah: Mercury is called the messenger of the gods (*gods* in Hebrew is *elohim*). They will prepare the way for the Messiah, just like John the Baptist did:

Mat 17:11 And Yeshua answered and said unto them, Elijah truly shall first come, and restore all things.

Mat 17:12 But I say unto you, That Elijah is come already[179], and they knew him not, but have done unto him whatever they listed. Likewise shall also the Son of man suffer of them.

Mat 17:13 Then the disciples understood that he spoke unto them of Yochanan the Baptist.

Then the King will return: Leo was following behind Mars and Mercury as they were setting.

---

[178] See *Venus and Jupiter conjunction: The 'Star of Bethlehem'* on page 52.

[179] Biblical history is prophetic, and prophecies often have multiple partial fulfilments until the final completion. This is a very important aspect of prophecies that must always be considered when reading Bible history and prophecy.

When Jesus said that Elijah shall first come, he was referring to the rise of prophets which, just like Elijah, will warn the people and preach repentance at the end of days. It is believed that the two prophets who will prophecy at the end of days will be Moses and Elijah (Rev 11).

The four living beings and the presence of God

The four living beings are associated with the presence of God and Jesus.

Jesus and the four living beings:

> *Eze 1:26 And above the firmament that was over their heads was the likeness of a throne, as the appearance of a sapphire stone: and upon the likeness of the throne was the* **likeness as the appearance of a man** *above upon it.*

> *Eze 1:28 As the appearance of the bow that is in the cloud in the day of rain, so was the appearance of the brightness round about. This was the appearance of the likeness of the glory of Yahweh. And when I saw it, I fell upon my face, and I heard a voice of one that spoke.*

> *Heb 1:3 And He (Yeshua) is the radiance of His (God's) glory and the exact representation of His nature*

There are two verses in the Bible where all four constellations of Aquarius are mentioned:

> *Rev 4:7 And the first being was like a lion, and the second being like a calf, and the third being had a face as a man, and the fourth being was like a flying eagle.*

> *Eze 1:10 As for the likeness of their faces, they four had the face of a man, and the face of a lion, on the right side: and they four had the face of an ox on the left side; they four also had the face of an eagle.*

The four banners around the Tabernacle also had these symbols:

> *Num 2:2 Every man of the children of Israel shall pitch by his own standard, with the ensign of their father's house: far off about the tabernacle of the congregation shall they pitch.*

> *Num 2:3a And on the east side toward the rising of the sun shall they of the standard of the camp of Judah pitch*

Num 2:10a On the south side shall be the standard of the camp of Reuben according to their armies

Num 2:18a On the west side shall be the standard of the camp of Ephraim according to their armies

Num 2:25a The standard of the camp of Dan shall be on the north side by their armies

Their banners were as follows:

Judah: Lion
Reuben: Man
Ephraim: Bull
Dan: Eagle

The Israelites camped around the Tabernacle, with the 4 symbols on their banners. God tabernacled with them. One of the names of Jesus is "Immanuel". It means "God with us".

The Tabernacle was erected and the priests were consecrated on 1 Aviv - the date of birth of Jesus. That is very significant. The Tabernacle and the priestly service are all pointing towards Jesus.

We expect Jesus to return at the Feast of Trumpets.[180] The Bible says that God will tabernacle with us. We also find another reference to *the fountain of water* during the Messianic Age in the following passage:

> *Rev 21:3 And I heard a great voice out of heaven saying: Behold,* **the tabernacle of God is with men**, *and He will dwell with them, and they shall be his people, and God himself shall be with them, and be their God.*

> *Rev 21:6 And he said unto me: It is done. I am the Aleph and the Tav, the beginning and the end. I will give unto him who is athirst of* **the fountain of the water of life** *freely.*

---

[180] See *The Bridegroom will return with the sound of the trump* on page 88.

Some astrologers and theologians believe that Ezekiel's vision of a "wheel within a wheel" was astronomical language and that it refers to the celestial equator and the ecliptic plane. That is not true, because Ezekiel mentions that there are 4 wheels, each one next to a cherub (Eze 10:9+20).

Some people believed that Ezekiel and John saw an astrological cherub, called a "lamassu", but it does not match exactly what they saw.

Portal Guardian from the ancient city of Calah (modern Nimroud). It guarded the palace of Ashurnasirpal's palace (c. 880 BC). Calah was one of the cities that Nimrod build (Gen 10:11).

This lamassu has the body of a lion, wings of an eagle, face of a man and the horns of a bull.

It is possible that its origins come from Nimrod. He established astrolatry and it is possible that it is a cherub based on the four cardinal points, but we don't know that for sure.

One possibility is that it represents the Age of Taurus (it has the same cardinal points as the Age of Aquarius, but with the vernal equinox at Taurus).

WC: Metropolitan Museum of Art

What is important to note is that the appearance of the 4 signs/beasts were prophetic and pointing towards the end times (Ezekiel and Revelations are end times prophetic books).

Just as the four signs were the cardinal points at the start of our world starting with Adam, so they have now returned to proclaim the coming of the second Adam, Jesus:

1 Cor 15:45 And so it is written: "The first man, Adam, became a living soul." The last Adam (Yeshua) became the quickening Spirit.

*Rev 5:6 And I beheld, and, lo, in the midst of the throne and of **the four living beings**, and in the midst of the elders, stood a Lamb as it had been slain, having seven horns and seven eyes, which are the seven Spirits of God sent forth into all the earth.*

The prophet Ezekiel also prophesied about a stream of water that will flow from the Temple (Eze 47). This will be the last Temple. It will be during the Messianic Age. This stream of water also supports the view that the Age of Aquarius is the Messianic Age.

He is the Son of Man, the Lion of Judah. He referred to himself as a Spring of Living Waters. He is the real Aquarius, and the Messianic Age will be the real New Age.

Signs in the heavens in the end times

Astronomical events like conjunctions are very common and are not signs in themselves that tell us anything. However, when conjunctions between certain planets and stars occur in specific constellations on specific dates, they often are signs or messages from God.

The big celestial clock is speaking to us who are living today: it is pointing towards the soon coming Messianic New Age, when Jesus will return as the Messiah and rule his Messianic Kingdom.

> Luk 21:25 And there shall be signs in the sun, and in the moon, and in the stars[181]; and upon the earth distress of nations, with perplexity; the sea and the waves roaring.

> Mat 24:30 And then shall appear the sign of the Son of man in heaven: and then shall all the tribes of the earth mourn, and they shall see the Son of man coming in the clouds of heaven with power and great glory.

Not only did God create the celestial bodies so that we can determine his appointments with us (Lev 23), He also created them as signs to tell us about the two most important events in the universe: the first and second coming of his Son. Astronomical events at the time of birth of Jesus confirmed his date of birth, just as astronomical events also points to his return.

The celestial bodies are the work of God's hands –
and He uses them to speak to us!

---

[181] The word "stars" also include the planets (planets were called "wandering stars").

Part 6: Controversial / debatable issues

Alexander Hislop: *The Two Babylons*

My main sources for "Astronomy and religion" were "*On Isis and Osiris*" (*Plutarch's Morals*),[182] *Asherah in the Hebrew Bible and Northwest Semitic Literature,*[183] *Temples and Priests of Sol in the City of Rome*[184] and *Ancient Mesopotamian Gods and Goddesses.*[185]

Readers who are familiar with *The Two Babylons* probably wondered why I went through all the trouble to do my own research, when I could have just quoted Hislop. The problem is that he is not regarded as a reliable source. Some critics claim that his conclusions are overly stretched or just plainly wrong.[186] Others say that his sources are fake. Even some Christian chat rooms and forums warn against Hislop and "Hislopites".[187]

It seems as if he merged all the myths into one. According to Hislop many deities (including Tammuz) were the same person as Nimrod, and he was married to Semiramis. Critics usually make reference to the fact that Semiramis lived centuries AFTER Nimrod, and therefore Hislop is wrong. Hislop says that there was another Semiramis "in the primeval ages of the world".

---

[182] "*On Isis and Osiris*". *Plutarch's Morals: Theosophical Essays*, translated by Charles William King, [1908].

[183] John Day (1986). "Asherah in the Hebrew Bible and Northwest Semitic Literature". *Journal of Biblical Literature*, Vol. 105, No. 3 (Sep., 1986)

[184] Hijmans, S. (2010). Temples and Priests of Sol in the City of Rome. Mouseion: *Journal of the Classical Association of Canada*. (PDF)

[185] The Ancient Mesopotamian Gods and Goddesses Project.
 Online (11/2018): [http://oracc.museum.upenn.edu/amgg/index.html]

[186] I have to agree. Because of his agenda and eagerness to prove that the customs and doctrines of the RCC come from Babylonian paganism his conclusions are often biased and not always based on sufficient evidence.

He's not completely wrong: With the founding of the RCC by the councils of the Roman Empire all the religions within the Roman Empire were syncretized. That is why you find elements within the RCC that come from the Celtic, Egyptian, Greek and Babylonian pagan religions. That is also why it is called "Roman Catholic" ("Catholic" means *universal*).

[187] Somebody who claims that the RCC is based on "Babylonian mystery religion" and that Nimrod was married to Semiramis.

One of his reference[188] for this "older Semiramis" is Justin.[189] Justin wrote that Semiramis was married to Ninus, that she built Babylon and a wall around it with burnt brick, and that Ninus was the first to make war upon his neighbours.

Based on that Hislop equoted Ninus with Nimrod. I did not find any records that indicated that the name of Nimrod's consort was Semiramis. However, Ishtar was also called Zarpanit, and Zarpanit was the name of the consort of Marduk/Nimrod. And we know that Ishtar was the consort of Tammuz.

Due to sincretism we must be very careful to jump to any conclusions. There is no conclusive evidence to say with relative certainty that Nimrod was also called Tammuz and that Zarpanit was called Semiramis. Therefore we should not state it as fact. The evidence seems to indicate that Semiramis ruled during the Assyrian Empire, much later than the time of Nimrod.

The one conclusion of Hislop that we can say for certainty is wrong is the following[190]:

"How, then, did the Romish Church fix on December the 25th as Christmas-day? Why, thus: Long before the fourth century, and long before the Christian era itself, a festival was celebrated among the heathen at that precise time of the year, in honour of the birth of the son of the Babylonian queen of heaven, and it may fairly be presumed that, in order to conciliate the heathen and to swell the number of the nominal adherents of Christianity, the same festival was adopted by the Roman Church, giving it only the name of Christ."[191]

---

[188] Alexander Hislop (1858). *The Two Babylons or The Papal Worship Proved to be the Worship of Nimrod and His Wife*. p.24
Online (12/2018): https://archive.org/details/theTwoBabylons/page/n23

[189] Marcus Junianus Justinus (1st century AD). *Epitome of the Philippic History of Pompeius Trogus*. Translated by John Selby Watson. pp.1-2
Online (12/2018): [http://www.forumromanum.org/literature/justin/english/trans1.html]

[190] Hislop (1858/93): Chapter 3, Festivals, Section I. Christmas and Lady-day [https://archive.org/details/theTwoBabylons/page/n91]

[191] The Protestants also have pagan customs and doctrines. The Reformers were still Catholics, they were just protesting some of the customs and doctrines. Other Catholic doctrines and customs they kept. (According to the Catholics the Protestants are "accepting the authority of the pope by observing Sunday".)

There was no "son of the Babylonian queen of heaven" born on 25 December who was the origin of Christmas:

- Horus was the son of Isis, the Egyptian queen of heaven, and he was born on the winter solstice (22 or 23 December).
- Tammuz was reborn at every vernal equinox.
- The Feast of Sol (the Roman sun god) was celebrated on 11 December.
- The Roman Mithras only came into existence near the end of the 1st century AD. He was merged with Sol and his birthday was moved to 25 December in order to get the Christians to celebrate it - Mithras Sol was the copycat of Jesus, NOT the other way round.
- The only sun deity that I know of whose birthday was probably celebrated on 25 December since ancient times was Belenus, the sun god from Celtic Mythology (Yule).

(I don't think that we can blame Hislop that he came to the conclusion that Christmas was derived from pagan festivals, because it has been taken over by pagan customs.)

The bottom line is that everything that Hislop wrote should not be taken as fact:

Ralph Woodrow wrote a book called *Babylon Mystery Religion*, based on *The Two Babylons* of Alexander Hislop. When he "began to hear rumblings that Hislop was not a reliable historian" he went back to Hislop's work to carefully investigate it.

He withdrew his book from print, because he could not "in good conscience continue to publish a book against pagan mixture knowing that it contained a mixture itself of misinformation about Babylonian origins".[192]

In Hislop's defence we can say that he worked without the help of "Dr. Google", and also that a lot of discoveries was made after he published his work.

It is advisable to check his references and to rather quote from that. His book is useful in the sense that it can make you aware of certain pagan customs and beliefs.

---

[192] You can read his story at this link: [https://www.equip.org/article/the-two-babylons/]

Astrology

The Bible makes a clear distinction between signs in the heavens (astronomical events with a message) and astrology. Astrology is the study of the movements and relative positions of celestial objects as a means for divining information about human affairs (horoscopes). There is no connection between astronomy and astrology.

Stars are a sign that it is night, they don't cause the night. Astrology is like believing that the stars caused the night. Since ancient times pagan priests studied astronomy in order to practice astrology (for them it was the same thing, two sides of a coin).

It is a pagan occult practice based on superstition. Astrologers claim that it works but there are no evidence to support it. Even the star signs used for the horoscopes of most people (more than 80%!) are not correct for the following reasons:

- Horoscopes are based on the 12 ancient zodiac signs, but there actually are 13 signs. The Babylonians left out the 13th sign of the Zodiac (Ophiuchus the Serpent Bearer) because it didn't corresponded so nicely with their calendar.[193]
- The constellations move because of their precession (backward moving) on the equinoxes. The dates given to determine people's zodiac signs are based on what they were in the days of the ancient Babylonians.

People living in the polar regions don't even have horoscope readings (unless they use some manipulations tricks).

The so-called "guidance" of the horoscopes is so vague and generic that it doesn't matter which month's you read anyway. Some people believe in horoscopes because their "predictions" are *sometimes* correct, but that is only because of mathematical probability. You can make any generic prediction to a group of people and it is guaranteed that some of it will happen.

---

[193] Ophiuchus is actually your real Zodiac sign if you are born between 29 November and 18 December.

Celestial bodies don't determine the circumstances in our lives. Our lives are governed by our decisions and by God. God mocks those who believe in astrology:

Isa 47:13 Thou are tired of all the consultations with your many counselors. Now let your astrologers, the stargazers who divide the heavens and make monthly predictions, stand up and save thee from the things that shall come upon thee.

Isa 47:14 Behold, they shall be as stubble; the fire shall burn them. They shall not deliver themselves from the power of the flame. There shall not be a coal to warm at, nor a fire to sit before.

It is an occult practice and forbidden by God:

Deu 18:10 There shall not be found among you any one ... that uses divination, or an observer of times.

Jer 10:2 Thus says Yahweh, Learn not the way of the heathen, and be not dismayed at the signs of heaven; for the heathen are dismayed at them.

Astrology was very important to the pagans of the Roman Empire, but it was not practised by early believers. It seems that astrologers also played a role in their persecution:

"From the start the Christian Church strongly opposed the false teachings of astrology. The Fathers energetically demanded the expulsion of the Chaldeans who did so much harm to the State and the citizens by employing a fantastic mysticism to play upon the ineradicable impulses of the common people, keeping their heathen conceptions alive and fostering a soul-perplexing cult which, with its fatalistic tendencies created difficulties in the discernment of right and wrong and weakened the moral foundations of all human conduct.

There was no room in the early Christian Church for followers of this pseudo-science. The noted mathematician Aquila Ponticus was expelled from the Christian communion about the year 120, on account of his astrological heresies.

The early Christians of Rome, therefore, regarded the astrological as their bitterest and, unfortunately, their too powerful enemies; and the astrologers probably did their part in stirring up the cruel persecutions of the Christians".[194]

Paul reprimanded the Galatians who returned to their practising of astrology:

Gal 4:8-10 Howbeit then, when you knew not God, you did service unto them which by nature are no gods. v9 But now, after that you have known God, or rather are known of God, how turn you again to the weak and beggarly elements, whereunto you desire again to be in bondage? V10 You observe days, and months, and times, and years

The Galatians were ex-pagans (verse 8). They did not celebrate the Biblical festivals before their conversion, so they could not return to them (verse 9). They celebrated the pagan festivals that were governed by astrology, which were the only things that they could return to. (See also Col 2:8)

The early church considered astrology to be a form of astrolatry (the worship of stars and other heavenly bodies as deities, or the association of deities with heavenly bodies):

Tertullian (c.155 - c.240 AD): "We observe among the arts also some professions liable to the charge of idolatry. Of astrologers, there should be no speaking even; . . . One proposition I lay down: that those angels, the deserters of God [demons] . . . were likewise the discoverers of this curious art [astrology], on that account also condemned by God"[195]

Clement of Alexandria (150 – 215 AD): "Therefore the astrologers, being ignorant of such mysteries, think that these things [the disasters brought about when demons inspire human sin] happen by the courses of the heavenly bodies; hence also, in their answers to those who go to them and consult them as to future things, they are

---

[194] The Catholic Encyclopedia, Vol. II, *Astrology under Christianity*
[195] Idolatry 9 [A.D. 211]

deceived in very many instances. Nor is it to be wondered at, for they are not prophets; but, by long practice, the authors of errors find a sort of refuge in those things by which they were deceived, and introduce certain 'climacteric periods,' that they may pretend a knowledge of uncertain things.

For they represent these 'climacterics' as times of danger, in which one sometimes is destroyed, sometimes is not destroyed, not knowing that it is not the course of the stars but the operation of demons that regulates these things; and those demons, being anxious to confirm the error of astrology, deceive men to sin by mathematical calculations, so that when they suffer the punishment of sin, either by the permission of God or by legal sentence, the astrologer may seem to have spoken the truth"

"As usually happens when men see unfavorable dreams, and can make nothing certain out of them, when any event occurs, then they adapt what they saw in the dream to what has occurred; so also is the mathematics of astrology. For before anything happens, nothing is declared with certainty; but after something has happened, they gather the causes of the event. And thus often, when they have been at fault, and the thing has fallen out otherwise, they take the blame to themselves, saying that it was such and such a star which opposed, and that they did not see it; not knowing that their error does not proceed from their unskillfulness in their art, but from the inconsistency of the whole system . . .

But we who have learned the reason of this mystery know the cause since, having freedom of will, we sometimes oppose our desires and sometimes yield to them. And therefore the issue of human doings is uncertain, because it depends upon freedom of will . . .

And this is why ignorant astrologers have invented to themselves the talk about 'climacterics' as their refuge in uncertainties".[196]

Astrology has a negative impact on our free will.

---

[196] The Recognitions of Clement 9:12, 10:12 [A.D. 221]

Christmas

The real date of birth of Jesus was on 5 April. This chapter is about traditional celebrations of Christmas, mostly on 25 December.

The reason why many writers come to the conclusion that Christmas is of pagan origin, is because it became a pagan celebration. (It probably would be more correct to say that people are celebrating Yuletide and Saturnalia while calling it "Christmas"!).

When I started my research on this project I ignored those articles which mentioned the Christian origins of Christmas, because I believed that it was fabricated stories. But as I learned more and more I slowly realized that the origins of celebrating Christmas on 25 December DOES have a Christian non-pagan origin.

Early believers who celebrated it focused on Jesus (like some of our devoted Christian ancestors did in the not too distant past). That is actually what we should be doing - IF we claim that we are celebrating the birthday of Jesus.

The 25 December date

The traditional dates of 25 December and 6 January that some ancient writers mentioned[197] were based on the belief that Miryam became pregnant on 25 March. The 6 January date is based on the same belief, but it comes from Greek scholars who used the first Greek spring month (Artemisios), instead of the first Hebrew spring month (Aviv) to determine Passover. This Greek date is proof of the Passover origin of the traditional dates.

In about 175 AD Theophilus of Caesarea was apparently instructing people to celebrate the birthday of Jesus on 25 December.[198]

---

[197] See *Calendars and the traditional dates of birth of Jesus* on page 58

[198] Rudolfp Hospinian (1612). *De origine Festorum Chirstianorum*, cited online at [http://www.dec25th.info/Objections%20Answered.html]. Online (12/2018): [https://play.google.com/store/books/details/Festa_Christianorum_Hoc_est_de_origine_ progressu_c?id=WDxfzV2fpeAC].

The traditional dates for Christmas (25 December and 6 January) were established by 221 AD.

In 274 AD the Sol Invictus ("Undefeated sun") cult became an official Roman cult. They celebrated "Dies Natalis Invicti Solis" ("the Birthday of the Undefeated sun") on 25 December. The Sol Invictus cult was just a continuation and revival of the Roman cult of Sol (sometimes called "Sol Indiges").

The traditional feast days of Sol were 8 August, 28 August and 11 December. These dates were unrelated to any seasonal astronomical event. Furthermore, the Romans had a lunisolar calendar until the Julan solar calendar of 46 BC. Only then did it become possible to celebrate recurring astronomical events on a fixed calendar date. But still the Roman ritual calendars (called "fasti") did not show any connection between the dates of the solstices and equinoxes and religious festivals.

There is no evidence of Roman religious festivals celebrated on the winter solstices prior to the 4th century AD.[199]

"Until the reigns of the sun-worshipping emperors Elagabalus (AD 218-222) and Aurelian (AD 270-275) when 25 December was chosen as *Dies Natalis Solis Invicti* apparently in the mistaken belief that that was the date of the Winter Solstice, the only Roman festival which seems to have been associated with an equinox or solstice was *Fors Fortuna* on 24 June (see W. Warde Fowler, 1899)".[200]

The facts show clearly that the date of 25 December to celebrate Christmas was not based on a Roman pagan festival - it was the other way round!

---

[199] Hijmans, S. (2010). Temples and Priests of Sol in the City of Rome. Mouseion: *Journal of the Classical Association of Canada*. 10. 381-427. 10.1353/mou.2010.0073.
Online (11/2018): [https://www.researchgate.net/publication/242330197_Temples_and_Priests_of_Sol_in_the_City_of_Rome]

[200] William Matthew O'Neil (1976). *Time and the Calendars* (Manchester University Press) p.85

"As Wallraff (2001: 175) has pointed out, it is quite possible that the mid-fourth century pagan celebration of the winter solstice had arisen in response to the Christian claim of December 25th as the birthday of Christ a quarter century or so earlier. In general, the extent to which late pagan festivals copied, incorporated, or responded to Christian practices and celebrations deserves more attention than it has received".[201]

The main celebration dates for Saturnalia was from 17 to 19 December: On 17 December there was a public banquet. 18 and 19 December were public holidays and the time when gifts were exchanged.

Christmas[202] and Yule are celebrated on the same day, but they have different origins and are not related. If you look at a "interfaith-calendar"[203] you will see quite a few "holy days" of different religions that are on the same day, but not related at all.[204]

> We always need to look for evidence of a shared origin,
> or for evidence that something indeed
> did originate from something else,
> BEFORE we can make conclusions about a connection.

The bottom line is this: it is a Biblical principle that we must have PROOF before we accuse somebody of anything. Speculation is not proof of anything, neither to quote the mistake of somebody (e.g. Hislop).

We cannot accuse somebody of idolatry when they celebrate Christmas with the focus on Jesus. However, if they are Christians and follow pagan customs then we should warn them against it.

---

[201] Hijmans, S. (2010). Temples and Priests of Sol in the City of Rome. p.15

[202] Real Christmas - NOT a Yule/Saturnalia celebration that is deceptively called "Christmas"!

[203] E.g. [http://www.interfaith-calendar.org]
"Interfaith" is an euphemism for "syncretism", i.o.w. paganism.

[204] Even feasts with the same names are also not necessarily related: both Chanukah and Diwali (a Hindu festival) are also called "Festival of Lights", but they are not related in any way whatsoever.

The origins of the "pagan Christmas"

In 325 AD Christianity became the state religion of the Roman Empire. That was the death of the early church. Constantine, the Roman emperor, was a devoted follower of Sol-Mithras the Roman sun god. He was only a Christian in name. He divorced the Church from her Hebrew roots and married her to paganism.

Pagans flooded the church because they were forced to by official decrees. But they were still pagans who didn't know Jesus. Their response was to give "Christian" names to their pagan deities and to call their pagan temples "churches". Their worship didn't change much. They still prayed to their idols, they just called them by the names of the "saints".

They also brought with them their pagan celebrations of *Yuletide* and *Dies Natalis Solis Invicti* on 25 December. That is where the "pagan Christmas" comes from.

Most people have since replaced the "Christian components" of "Christmas", even though many still call it "Christmas". The honest ones who know what it really is about (e.g. Wiccans) call it "Yule".

Are you celebrating Yule or Christmas?

The difference between celebrating Yule (a pagan festival) and Christmas (originally a Christian festival) lies in what you do on that day: if the focus is on the birth of Jesus, and you read the Bible story and sing Christmas carols then you are celebrating Christmas.

However, if Jesus is barely mentioned (or not at all) and the focus is on pagan rituals, then you are actually celebrating Yule and practising paganism.

God hates it when we try to serve Him like the pagans serve their gods:

> *Exo 32:35 And Yahweh plagued the people, because they made the calf, which Aharon made.*

Jer 10:2-4 Thus says Yahweh, Learn not the way of the heathen, and be not dismayed at the signs of heaven; for the heathen are dismayed at them. v3 For the customs of the people are vain: for one cuts a tree out of the forest, the work of the hands of the workman, with the axe. v4 They deck it with silver and with gold; they fasten it with nails and with hammers, that it move not.

Jer 16:19 Yahweh, my strength, and my fortress, and my refuge in the day of affliction, the Gentiles shall come unto thee from the ends of the earth, and shall say, Surely our fathers have inherited lies, vanity, and things wherein there is no profit.

Col 2:8 Beware lest any man spoil you through philosophy and vain deceit, after the tradition of men, after the rudiments of the world, and not after the Messiah.[205]

Yuletide and the "Christmas tree"

Hesse in Germany is an old gathering place for witches. One of their traditions was to dance around a fir tree and then set it ablaze. Hessian soldiers brought the practice of decorating a fir tree to America during the American Revolution.

In the 1840's Queen Victoria asked her German husband, Prince Albert, to decorate a tree like he did in his childhood. A sketch of it featured in the *Illustrated London News*. Queen Victoria was very popular, so it immediately became highly fashionable in Britain and America.[206]

It is believed that Martin Luther, the 16th-century protesting Roman Catholic from Germany, first added lighted candles to a tree. Luther came from Hesse (Today there are trained "pilgrim guides" that will take you on the "Luther Trail in Hesse).[207]

---

[205] See also *Paul reprimanded the Galatians who returned to their practising of astrology* on page 122

[206] www.history.com/topics/christmas/history-of-christmas-trees

[207] www.luther2017.de/en/experience/luther-trails/the-luther-trail-in-hesse/

Pagan "Christmas trees"

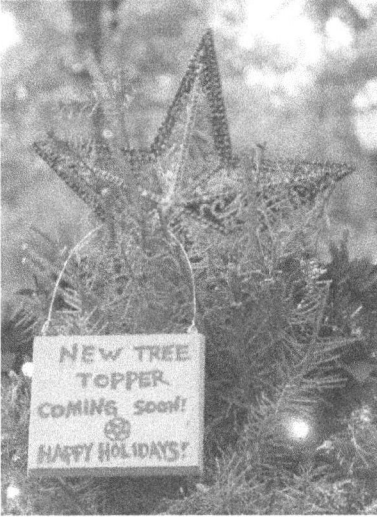

Even Satanists have "Christmas trees" (they know it's origin).

On the evening of 25 November 2017 the head topper of this "Christmas tree" was stolen. It was a big goat head mask.[208]

It belonged to the local Satanic temple in San Jose, California.

It was part of their display for the annual "Christmas in the Park" event.

In the void left by the large black goat head mask they put a red star and a wood-engraved sign to inform visitors that a new topper was "coming soon".

Pauline Campanelli (a practicing Wiccan witch) writes the following[209]:

"Some of the most wonderful traditions practiced by our parents and grandparents are purely Pagan in origin. So go ahead and celebrate the customs of your childhood. Send Valentines, dye Eostre's eggs, bring a fir tree into your house and decorate it with ornaments that came down in the family, and know in your Pagan heart that what you do is a traditional way of honouring the Old Pagan Gods.

And when someone says to you, "I thought you were a Pagan. Why do you have a Christmas tree in your house?"

You can look them straight in the face and say,

"Because it's a Pagan tradition – why do you?

---

[208][https://www.mercurynews.com/2017/11/29/goat-head-topper-stolen-from-san-jose-satanist-grou ps-christmas-tree/] Image: Jason Green, Bay Area News Group (cropped)
[209] Pauline Campanelli, *Ancient Ways – Reclaiming Pagan Tradition* (Llewelly Publications, 1995), 220

Who is Santa Claus?

Santa Claus is basically the "Yule goat", blended with Odin/Woden who is wearing the red clothes and hat of Sol Invictus-Mithras. Other deities are also syncretized with him, e.g. Father Frost, the Oak King (fertility god, the Green Man) and the Holly[210] King (god of transformation), etcetera. He was also syncretized with the Lord of Misrule[211].

Odin[212] climbed down chimneys to give gifts to children. They filled their boots with straw for Sleipnir[213] and set them by the hearth.

Joulupukki ("Yule goat") was the Finnish gift bringer at Yule. He was a goat-man with horns and hooves.[214] He wore red leather pants and a fur trimmed red leather coat. He traveled in a sleigh pulled by a number of reindeer (they could not fly like those of Santa).

The birthday of Mithras was on 25 December. On paintings he is depicted with red clothes and a red Mithras cap - just like Santa!

Santa's sleigh

His sleigh can be traced back to the various modes of transport of pagan gods: the barks (sacred boats) of the Egyptian deities[215], the chariot of Sol, Helios, Apollo or Thor, and Sleipnir the steed of Odin.

---

[210] The Druids believed that holly will protect against evil spirits. Harry Potter's magic wand is made from holly wood.

[211] See 17-23 December: Saturnalia on page 34

[212] King of the Norwegian gods. He was the lord of Alfheim, home of the elves. Some Christians say "Put Christ back in Christmas". The pagans say "Don't take Odin out of Yule". Online (2018):

[https://www.norwegianamerican.com/featured/dont-take-odin-out-of-yule/]

[213] The eight-legged steed of Odin

[214] Maybe that is why some Satanists put a goat head mask on their Yule tree.

[215] Especially Ra and Horus

May we celebrate a Christian Christmas?

I'm referring to a celebration where Jesus is the centre, one without the pagan customs.[216]

Some people object to the celebrating of Christmas. They say that we are not commanded to do it in Scripture. That is true, but we are not forbid to do things to the honour of God. People do many things to the glory of God, without being told to do it:

David and Miryam danced, Pinchas killed a defiant idolater, Chanukah (Feast of Dedication) and Purim (Feast of Esther) honours God for saving the Jews, etcetera.

I'm not saying that you should or should not, but whatever you decide to do make sure that it honours God:

> *Rom 14:6a He who observes the (non-scriptural feast or fast) day, observes it unto Yahweh; and he who does not observe the (non-scriptural feast or fast) day, to Yahweh he does not observe it.*

On which day should be celebrate Christmas?

Some people say that it doesn't really matter when we celebrate the birthday of Jesus, it is the thought that counts. What would you say if somebody celebrated your birthday on another day while knowing the real day?

To celebrate the birthday of Jesus on 1 Aviv (Nissan), the first day of the Jewish year, has spiritual and symbolic meaning. Our celebrations should focus on Jesus our Messiah, the Word who became flesh. We can reflect on who and what Jesus really is:

- He is our King: Jewish regnal years started on 1 *Aviv*.
- He is our High Priest: The Tabernacle and priests were dedicated on 1 Aviv.
- He must be our priority – 1 *Aviv* first day of spiritual year.
- The day reminds us of his return.

---

[216] See *Christian or pagan celebrations: Your choice* on page 49

Appendixes

Appendix A: Some sources for more information:

- Gérard Gertoux, *Herod the Great and Jesus - Chronological, Historical and Archaeological Evidence*, (Lulu.com, 2017)

- Schaff, Philip: *History of the Christian Church - From the 1st to the 19th century* (PDF version, available from the "Christian Classics Ethereal Library" at www.ccel.org).

- Filmer, W. E. "Chronology of the Reign of Herod the Great", *Journal of Theological Studies* no 17 (1966), 283–298.

- Edwards, Ormond. "Herodian Chronology", Palestine Exploration Quarterly 114 (1982) 29–42

- Keresztes, Paul. *Imperial Rome and the Christians: From Herod the Great to About 200 CE* (Lanham, Maryland: University Press of America, 1989), pp.1–43.

- Martin, Ernest L., "The Nativity and Herod's Death": Vardaman, Jerry and Yamauchi, Edwin M., eds. (1989). *Chronos, Kairos, Christos: Nativity and Chronological Studies*. Presented to Jack Finegan. Winona Lake, Indiana: Eisenbrauns: 85–92).

- Finegan, Jack. *Handbook of Biblical Chronology*, Rev. ed. (Peabody, MA: Hendrickson, 1998) 300, §516.

- Steinmann, Andrew "When Did Herod the Great Reign?", *Novum Testamentum*, Volume 51, Number 1, 2009, pp. 1–29.

- "On Isis and Osiris". Plutarch's Morals: Theosophical Essays, tr. by Charles William King, [1908].
Online (12/2018): [http://www.sacred-texts.com/cla/plu/pte/pte04.htm]

- John Day (1986). "Asherah in the Hebrew Bible and Northwest Semitic Literature". Journal of Biblical Literature, Vol. 105, No. 3 (Sep., 1986). Online (11/2018): [https://www.jstor.org/stable/3260509]

- Hijmans, S. (2010). Temples and Priests of Sol in the City of Rome. Mouseion: Journal of the Classical Association of Canada. (PDF)
Online (11/2018): [https://www.researchgate.net/publication/242330197_Temples_and_Priests_of_Sol_in_the_City_of_Rome]

- The Ancient Mesopotamian Gods and Goddesses Project.
Funded by the UK Higher Education Academy's Subject Centre for History, Classics, and Archaeology in 2009-2010. Online (11/2018): [http://oracc.museum.upenn.edu/amgg/index.html]

Appendix B: Names and associations of deities

It all began with the Sumerians. The gods and goddesses of mythology were powerful rulers who were deified.

People believed that the deities of other cultures were the same deities as theirs, just with different names. They paired and syncretized deities with more or less similar powers and attributes. (They also believed that it was more effective to invoke them by more than one name).

Babylonian deities were syncretized with Sumerian deities. They also replaced the names of their counterparts, e.g. Inanna became Ishtar. The same process took place between various cultures, e.g. Egyptian, Greek, Celtic etcetera.

Often their names were compounded: When Osiris died he merged with Ptah and Sokar and became Ptah-Sokar-Osiris (although Sokar was actually Horus his son, who was his reincarnation). Sol and Mithras became "Deus Sol Invictus Mithras".

Some associations are based on historical records. Others are based on similarities which seems to point to a common origin. Often the name of a deity in one culture is equated with various deities in other cultures, e.g. Dionysus is equated with Osiris, Horus and Tammuz.

Marduk = Nimrod

The signs for the name of Marduk can ideographically be read as Nimrod in Hebrew.[217] His name is transliterated AMAR.UD[218].

Sumerian cuneiform is consonantal (no vowels, just like Hebrew). The consonants for Marduk are MRD. The Hebrew word with those root letters is "Marad". It means "rebel", which clearly fits Nimrod. So how does that brings us by Nimrod? With the simple passive form of the verb ("niphal") the n-sound is added as a preposition, which gives us NMRD. Add the vowels and you get Nimrod.

---

[217] [http://jewishencyclopedia.com/articles/11548-nimrod]

[218] (Some spellings have the K-sound.)
[http://oracc.museum.upenn.edu/amgg/listofdeities/marduk/index.html]

The simple passive conjugation tells me that Nimrod was a rebel at heart, even if he did nothing. (I'm not a language expert so my conclusion could be wrong, but it's not only their names that connect them). They both ruled Babylon. It is recorded of both that they built a ziggurat in the city of Babylon.

Marduk-Nimrod-Osiris-Baal/Tammuz

Marduk/Nimrod can be associated with Baal, who is associated with Tammuz: One myth says that Marduk destroyed the sea god, another one says that it was Baal. Also, Zarpanit/Asherah was the name of the consort of Baal/Tammuz. Zarpanit was also the name of the consort of Marduk/Nimrod. Both Marduk and Tammuz were gods of agriculture.

Marduk/Nimrod can be associated with Osiris: Both were sun gods. Both were killed. Both were associated with bulls (The name Marduk can be interpreted as "calf of the sun", and Osiris is represented by the Apis bull). Both Nimrod and Osiris were black.

Tammuz / Seth / Moloch / Baal / Adon / Odin

Despite the parallels between the story of Baal's murder and resurrection with those of Osiris, the Baal worshipers in Egypt did not connect the two. Instead they associated him with Seth, the brother of Osiris, because they were both gods of storm.[219]

Tammuz was also associated with Moloch.[220] He is associated with Saturn because of agriculture. Saturn is associated with the end of the autumn planting season.

Tammuz is associated with Baal the consort of Asherah. She is associated with Hathor, the wife of Horus.

Odin[221] and Adonis is derived from Adon. Both Adon and Baal means "lord" or "master". Both of them were lamented.

---

[219] April McDevitt: [http://www.egyptianmyths.net/baal.htm]

[220] https://www.jewishvirtuallibrary.org/the-cult-of-moloch

[221] The change from Adon to Odin is called "vowel reduction". Vowels are also often used interchangeably.

The Queens of Heaven: Isis, Hathor and Ishtar

Isis[222] is called the *"Goddess with Ten Thousand Names"*. That is because she was worshiped by many names. Isis, Hathor and Ishtar were all called "Queen of Heaven". They were also "Cow Mother goddesses", because they were seen as mothers giving sustenance to their people.

Isis became the most dominant goddess in the world. She absorbed the roles and titles of many earlier Goddesses. She and her son Horus was probably the first *Madonna and child* to be worshiped (When Christianity came under Roman control, many statutes of them were just re-named Mary and Jesus).

Ishtar / Asherah / Hathor / Astarte / Anat

Ishtar[223] is the Babylonian name for Inanna. She is considered by some to be the same goddess as Hathor. Later on she was usually called Zarpanit. She was considered to be the wife of Bil-Marduk[224].

Asherah (Qudshu/Athirat) was independent from Astarte and Anat, but they later merged and became Qudshu-Astarte-Anat.[225] As Astarte she was the consort of Tammuz, as Anat she was the consort of Baal-Hadad. (This confirms Tammuz as one of the Baals who were worshiped in Israel).

In the city of Gebal there stood a temple for Astarte, so there they called her Baalat Gebal, *Lady of Gebal*. When the name of the city changed to Byblus she was called *Baalat Byblus*[226], Lady of Byblus.

---

[222] "On Isis and Osiris". Plutarch's Morals: Theosophical Essays, translated by Charles William King, [1908].

[223] http://oracc.museum.upenn.edu/amgg/listofdeities/inanaitar/index.html

[224] Barton, G. (1891). Ashtoreth and Her Influence in the Old Testament. *Journal of Biblical Literature*, 10(2), p. 76.

[225] John Day (1986). "Asherah in the Hebrew Bible and Northwest Semitic Literature". *Journal of Biblical Literature*, Vol. 105, No. 3 (Sep., 1986), p.385, 389

Online (11/2018): [https://www.jstor.org/stable/3260509]

[226] Baalat is the female form of Baal. Her name was not Gebal or Byblus, that was just part of her title to show that she was the deity of that city. It's like calling the Statue of Liberty "Baalat New York" (Lady of New York).

Appendix C: References for traditional birth dates

1. Lucas the Evangelist (c. 10 BC - 74 CE) (Luke 3:1-23, c70 CE): Jesus was about 30 years of age when he started his ministry, during the 15th year of reign of Tiberius Caesar (14 - 37 CE):
14 + 15 – 31 (no year zero) = -2 BC

Clement of Alexandria (c. 150 - 215 CE) confirms it[227]:

"And the followers of Basilides hold the day of his baptism as a festival, spending the night before in readings. And they say that it was the fifteenth year of Tiberius Cæsar, the fifteenth day of the month Tubi (10 January); and some that it was the eleventh of the same month (6 January)".

The shepherds didn't stay outside in winter, so we know that it was not in winter. Jesus was born at least a few months before the death of Herod (28 January 1 BC).

2. Clement goes further and adds 2 more dating reference points:

"From the birth of Christ, therefore, to the death of Commodus (31 December 192 CE) are, in all, a hundred and ninety-four years, one month, thirteen days (17 November 2 BC).

And there are those who have determined not only the year of our Lord's birth, but also the day; and they say that it took place in the twenty-eighth year of Augustus, and in the twenty-fifth day of (the Egyptian month) Pachon (20 May)".

194 years before death of Commodus (31 December 192 CE):
192 - 194 = -2 BC

The 28th year of the reign of Augustus (sole ruler):
-30 + 28 = -2 BC

---

[227] *Stromata XXI.145 (c 195 CE) – The Jewish Institutions and Laws of Far Higher Antiquity Than the Philosophy of the Greeks*

Many early believers believed that Jesus was baptized on the same day of his birth. Some Orthodox churches still celebrate his birth and baptism on 6 January.

3. Irenaeus of Lyons (c 130 - 202 CE)[228] :
41st year of reign of Augustus (October 43 BC): -43 + 41 = -2 BC

Note: Clement does his dating from 29 August 30 BC, after the Battle of Actium and the death of Cleopatra, when Augustus became the sole ruler. Other ancient writers (like Tertullian and Irenaeus) date the reign of Augustus from the forming of the second triumvirate (a coalition government) in October 43 BC.

4. Tertullian of Carthage (c.160 - 225 CE)[229]:
41st year of reign of Augustus (coalition, 43 BC): -43 + 41 = -2 BC
28 years after death of Cleopatra (Aug 30 BC): -30 + 28 = -2 BC

He calculates the period from the birth of Jesus to the destruction of Jerusalem as 52 years and 6 months. He miscalculated the years (he left out the reign of Claudius), but he must have been very much aware of the fact that the Jews commemorates the destruction of the Temple on the 9th of Av (July or August). That gives us January or February.

Tertullian also calculates the date of the baptism of Jesus to be 115 years and 6½ months before the coming of Marcion.[230] The heretical sect of Marcion was founded in July 144 CE. Tertullian links this event to the *aura canicularis*, "the wind of the dog-star" (Sirius or Sothis), which is dated 19th or 20th July. 6½ months before that takes us to the first week of January.

According to some traditions Jesus was baptised and born on the same day, and 6 January was one of the prevalent traditional dates for his birth.

5. Hippolytus of Rome (170 - 235 CE)[231]: in the year 5500 AM

---

[228] Irenaeus of Lyons (c. 180 CE). *Against Heresies* III: 21:3

[229] Tertullian of Carthage (c.200 CE). *Against the Jews* VIII:11:75

[230] Tertullian. *Against Marcion* 1:19

[231] Hippolytus of Rome (c.210 CE). *Commentary on Daniel*
He was a disciple of Irenaeus

Anno Mundi = 'year of the world' or since creation.[232] Africanus mentions that the commencement of the 250th Olympiad (221 CE) was 192 years after 5531 AM[233].

5531 AM = 221 − 192 = 29 CE. From 5500 to 5531 AM is 31 years. Therefore 5500 AM = 29 − 31 = 2 BC.

There are several manuscripts of Hippolytus' "Commentary on Daniel", one with two dates: 2 April and 25 December. It seems that 2 April was the original date which was "corrected" (the manuscripts are stored at the Vatican).

In the Vatican Museum is an ancient statue of Hippolytus. The dates of Passover for the years 222 to 333 is inscribed on it, and next to one of the dates (2 April) the words "genesis Christou" ("birth" of Christ) is inscribed.

In his *Chronicon Pashhale* Hippolytus writes that from the Passover of Ezra to the birth of Jesus is 563 years.

Clearly he believed that Jesus was born at Passover, which is either in March or April.

6. Sextus Julius Africanus (c. 170 - 250 CE)[234]: in the year 5500 AM

5500 AM = 2 BC (see explanation at top of page)

Sextus believed that Jesus was conceived on 25 March and born on 25 December.[235]

---

[232] Their "Anno Mundi" calendar does not match Biblical chronology

[233] Sextus Julius Africanus (221 CE). *Chronographiai*, fragment 18.4. According to him the year 5531 AM was the "coming" of Jesus, referring to the beginning of his ministry.

[234] Ibid.

[235] The date of 6 January mentioned by Clement and Tertulllian is also based on the tradition that Jesus was conceived on Pesach and born nine months later, but they used the 14th day of the Greek month Artemisios, which falls on 6 April on the Julian/Roman calendar. That is the origin of the 6 January date.

7. Origen Adamantius (c. 175 - 260 CE)[236]:

41st year of reign of Augustus (October 43 BC) : -43 + 41 = -2 BC

8. There is a third-century work called *De Pascha Computus* (c 243 CE) which is considered to be the work of Cyprian.[237] It says that the first day of creation coincided with the first day of spring on March 25th, and that Jesus was born four days later on the 28th on a Wednesday. (The sun was created on the 4th day, and Jesus is seen as the Sun of Righteousness.)

9. Eusebius of Caesarea (c. 260 - 340 CE):

28 years after death of Cleopatra[238]: -30 + 28 = -2 BC

In the third year of the 194th Olympiad[239]: -2 BC

10. Epiphanius of Salamis (c. 305 - 403 CE)[240]:

When Augustus XIII and Silvanus were consuls: 2 BC

He believed that Jesus was conceived on 6 April and born on 6 January, 9 months later.[241]

11. Jerome[242]: 49 years before the 8th year of Claudius Caesar

Claudius became emperor on 25 January 41 CE. His 7th year (the year before the 8th year) was 47 CE. Forty nine years before that is 2 BC.

12. Paulus Orosius[243] (c. 380 - 450 CE):
Year 752 from the founding of Rome

Rome was founded on 21st April 753 BC.
The 752th year ended on 20th April 1 BC.

---

[236] Origen Adamantius (231 CE): *Homily* (sermon) on Luke 3:1

[237] Some consider it to be a lost work of Hippolytus, but apparently Cyprian re-edits and corrects Hippolytus in it.

[238] Eusebius of Caesarea (340 CE). *Ecclesiastical History* I:5:2

[239] Eusebius of Caesarea (c. 325 CE). *Chronicle*

[240] Epiphanius of Salamis (357 CE). *Panarion* LI:22:3

[241] Thomas Talley, *The origins of the liturgical year* (Liturgical Press, 1986) p98

[242] Jerome (c.407 CE). *Commentary on Daniel*. He quotes Apollinaris (310 - 390 CE). Translated by Gleason Archer (1958 CE).

[243] Paulus Orosius (418 CE). *Histories against the pagans* VI:22.1

Appendix D: Born of a virgin: Is it possible?

A virgin birth is, from a scientific perspective, much more likely than evolution: According to the evolution theory, the first cell was formed by chance. Then miraculously that cell evolved by chance, creating new genetic code out of nowhere.

With a virgin birth you already have a living cell, all it needs is more genetic code. In nature we have examples of propagation without fertilization, e.g. drones (male bees), Komodo dragons, etcetera. This is called "parthenogenesis".

George Wald (biochemist and evolutionist) said the following[244]: "One has only to contemplate the magnitude of this task to conclude that the spontaneous generation of a living organism is impossible. Yet here we are -- as a result, I believe, of spontaneous generation."

That statement basically represents the belief of the evolutionists: "It is impossible, but it MUST have happened, because we exist". It is a statement of faith. Evolution is a religion, but evolutionists deny it, because it will hinder their cause.

What is science? Robert Krampf gives a good definition: "Science is an objective, self correcting method for gathering and organizing information about the natural world through repeated observation and experimentation"[245].

Because evolution cannot be proven scientifically, evolutionists have created their own definition, something like "Science is the search for natural solutions".

Antony Flew[246] (1923 - 2010) was a British philosophy professor. He was one of the world's most influential atheists. He became an atheist at the age of 15.

---

[244] George Wald (1955). "The Origins of Life," in *The Physics and Chemistry of Life* (Simon & Schuster, 1955), p.270

[245] https://thehappyscientist.com/content/definition-science

[246] https://creation.com/review-there-is-a-god-by-antony-flew
https://www.foxnews.com/story/leading-atheist-philosopher-concludes-gods-real

He said that the debate over God must begin by presuming atheism, putting the burden of proof on those arguing that God exists (1984, "The Presumption of Atheism"). He also said that his whole life has been guided by the principle of Plato's Socrates: "Follow the evidence, wherever it leads."

That is precisely what he did. Investigation of DNA convinced him that intelligence must have been involved. He also said that evolutionary theory has no reasonable explanation for "the first emergence of living from non-living matter"—that is, the origin of life". He published his findings in 2007.[247]

The only way to make an honest judgment about anything is to look at the evidence from all sides. If you are an atheist or skeptic, then I want to invite you to study some of "the burden of proof that God exists":

Some excellent books:
Dr. Jonathan Sarfati, Ph.D.
Refuting Evolution and *Refuting Evolution 2*

Some useful links:
[http://evolutionfacts.com]

[https://creation.com]

[http://www.gjcn.org/2009/09/the-great-hoax-of-evolution/]

[http://detectingdesign.com/quotesfromscientists.html]

[https://answersingenesis.org/evidence-against-evolution/probability/does-evolution-have-a-chance/]

[https://x-evolutionist.com]

[https://x-evolutionist.com/the-origin-of-life-how-did-life-begin-dna-could-not-have-happened-by-chance/]

[http://www.creationism.org/heinze/EvolutionReligion.htm]

[http://theoutlet.us/Quotesoncomplexityofcellandoriginoflife.pdf]

---

[247] Antony Flew with Roy Varghese (2007). *There is a God: How The World's Most Notorious Atheist Changed His Mind.* (Harper Collins, New York).

Appendix E : The "Jesus myth" hoax

"For those who believe, no proof is necessary.
For those who don't believe, no proof is possible."

— Stuart Chase

At first glance the statement above sounds true - but it is not. A true statement would be "For those who REFUSE to believe, no proof is possible". This is especially true for many atheists and fake atheists[248]. They fabricated the "Jesus myth" hoax.

They will try to convince people that Jesus is a myth based on other myths. Their "logic" is as follows: "There are some deities who have some similarities to Jesus, therefore Jesus MUST also be a myth".

(It's like saying that Divali (an Indian festival) and Chanukah (a Jewish festival) are related and that one MUST have developed from the other, JUST BECAUSE both of them are also called "Festival of Lights".)

The main reason why the hoax is still around is because of the censorship of the secular anti-christian activists that have taken over control of academic institutions.[249]

---

[248] Some Satanists will try to convince people that God does not exist. God is their enemy and they want to prevent them from worshiping Him.

[249] When a team of researchers dared to mention the word "Creator" in a paper about the biomechanical characteristics of hand coordination in the scientific journal PLOS ONE, one of the editors threatened to resign if the paper was not retracted immediately.
[https://creation.com/hand-design-peer-review]

When books that try to portray Jesus as just another myth is published, the mainstream academic world promotes it. Books that refute those claims are ignored. Online (12/1280): [http://www.redmoonrising.com/osiris.htm]

"Ben Stein's "Expelled: No Intelligence Allowed" is a movie about the freedom of speech suppression to which Intelligent Design proponents are being subjected to by the atheistic American academic dictatorship."
[https://www.youtube.com/watch?v=V5EPymcWp-g]

One of the comments on the page is "evolution is a fact".
REAL fact: No it is not! Evolution has been scientifically disproven.
(Ask the guys at https://creation.com if you need more evidence.)

Because there are similarities between the myths of "pagan saviors" and the story of Jesus, the atheists and anti-christians do their best to try and portray Jesus as just another myth. But if those myths are thoroughly studied and compared with the historical evidence and the gospels records,[250] then it becomes clear that the death and resurrection of Jesus is not based on any of those myths.[251]

Horus and Mithras

The 2 favourite "savior deities" of the atheists (and a few sceptics[252]) are probably Horus and the Roman Mithras. Their false claims can be easily refuted by any knowledgeable person who is critical and honest.[253]

The festivals for the rising of Osiris, the birth of Horus and Kikellia most probably were all on 23 December. According to the calculations of the Egyptians and Romans the winter solstice was on 25 December. But they used the Julian calendar. If they referred to the winter solstice, then it was on 23 December (according to our Gregorian calendar) at the time of Jesus.

However, if they specifically kept to their calendar date of 25 December on the Julian calendar, then the date for the festival slowly moved. (The Julian calendar has too many leap years. See also *The Vernal Equinox and April fools day* on page 24).

---

[250] Some antichristian "scholars" blatantly lie when they claim that there is no historical evidence that Jesus lived, or that the disciples really lived, or that they lived in the lifetime of Jesus.

Their bias is so great that they claim that Jesus was a myth, but not a historical figure - even though myths like Horus and Tammuz are based on real historical figures!

[251] http://www.redmoonrising.com/Giza/DyingandRising3.htm
http://www.redmoonrising.com/osiris.htm

[252] Most so-called "sceptics" are fake: They only question Christian and Biblical beliefs. They refuse to thoroughly investigate the scientific evidence against evolution. If they did few (if any) of them would believe in evolution.

[253] For a refutation of the claim that Horus was the prototype for Jesus:
Joshua J. Mark (2016) - "Horus & Jesus controversy": *Horus* (Ancient History Encyclopedia). Online (12/2018): https://www.ancient.eu/Horus/

For a refutation of the claim that Mithras was the prototype for Jesus, see *Feast of Sol (Roman)* on page 33.

Books feedback and orders

Books can be ordered from: orders@moadim.org.za

Contact author at gerhardmoadim@gmail.com for feedback and questions. Or visit our Facebook page:

https://web.facebook.com/starmessengers/

This book is also available as a Kindle eBook on Amazon.com

Hierdie boek is ook in Afrikaans beskikbaar onder die volgende titel:

"Die Sterboodskappers - Verkondigers van tye en tekens"

About our articles and teachings

Teachings and resources posted on our website can be downloaded for free.

It may be copied and distributed on the condition that it is done without alterations, with reference to the source.

https://www.moadim.org.za/en

Prayers and financial support are appreciated:

Bank details:
Acc Name: Moadim
Acc. No: 9232 262 409
ABSA savings account
Branch: Hermanus   632005

Thank you very much and God bless you!

Shalom

MOADIM
MEDIA

www.ingramcontent.com/pod-product-compliance
Lightning Source LLC
Chambersburg PA
CBHW051428090426
42737CB00014B/2874